Introduction to Polish Tax Law

Lex et Res Publica
Polish Legal and Political Studies
Edited by Anna Jaroń

Volume 8

Zur Qualitätssicherung und Peer Review der vorliegenden Publikation

Die Qualität der in dieser Reihe erscheinenden Arbeiten wird vor der Publikation durch die Herausgeberin der Reihe geprüft.

Notes on the quality assurance and peer review of this publication

Prior to publication, the quality of the work published in this series is reviewed by the editor of the series.

Marcin Burzec / Paweł Smoleń

Introduction to Polish Tax Law

PETER LANG

Bibliographic Information published by the Deutsche Nationalbibliothek
The Deutsche Nationalbibliothek lists this publication
in the Deutsche Nationalbibliografie; detailed bibliographic
data is available in the internet at http://dnb.d-nb.de.

Library of Congress Cataloging-in-Publication Data
Names: Burzec, Marcin, author. | Smolen, Pawe?, author.
Title: Introduction to Polish tax law / Marcin Burzec, Pawe? Smolen.
Description: Berlin ; New York : Peter Lang, 2018. | Series: Lex et Res
   publica Polish legal and political studies ; vol.8 | Includes
   bibliographical references.
Identifiers: LCCN 2018030971 | ISBN 9783631757406
Subjects: LCSH: Taxation--Law and legislation--Poland. | Tax administration
   and procedure--Poland. | Fiscal policy--Poland.
Classification: LCC KKP3550 .B87 2018 | DDC 343.43804--dc23 LC record
available at https://lccn.loc.gov/2018030971

Reviewed by Prof. Gianluca Selicato and Prof. Henryk Dzwonkowski.

ISSN 2191-3250
ISBN 978-3-631-75740-6 (Print)
E-ISBN 978-3-631-75969-1 (E-Book)
E-ISBN 978-3-631-75970-7 (EPUB)
E-ISBN 978-3-631-75971-4 (MOBI)
DOI 10.3726/b14482

© Peter Lang GmbH
International Academic Publishers
Berlin 2018
All rights reserved.

Peter Lang – Berlin· Bern · Bruxelles · New York ·
Oxford · Warszawa · Wien

This publication has been peer reviewed

www.peterlang.com

Foreword

Tax law is among the fastest-growing legal disciplines. It is an inherent part to any national legal system. Today, the proceeds of taxes collected by both the central and local governments have grown in importance dramatically. Suffice to say, they are the main source of budget revenues. By extension, taxes garner an avid interest of all the parties concerned.

A tax system is essentially made up of a variety of contributions applicable at a given time and in a given country and constituting a set of inter-related and mutually dependent elements creating an organised whole. To make such a system work efficiently is anything but an easy task. In practice, a tax system is the product of multiple and diverse ideas and operations that, as a matter of fact, reflects a compromise between some theoretical assumptions, feasible solutions, and budgetary needs.

Poland has seen the process of tax law reform going on for many years. The economic and political transformation at the turn of the 20th century determined the fundamental trends of the transformation of this area of law. Regrettably, it is not always possible to achieve the desired outcome of intended modifications. It is not infrequently that some new solutions are introduced hastily, on an ad hoc basis, and short-sightedly. This results in anything but an overwhelming sense of instability, which necessitates further changes to be put in place. A novelty in the Polish tax legislation is the need of incorporating, or aligning with, the legal standards required through the membership in the European Union. However, this law harmonisation process fails to address the whole of Polish tax law.

This book covers the fundamental areas of taxation and tax law in Poland. It explores the tax theory, general tax law, and specific taxes supplying the central and self-government budget revenues. The authors also seek to highlight some selected issues of the operation and evolution of Polish tax law.

Lublin, May 2018   *Marcin Burzec, Paweł Smoleń*

Contents

1 Taxes and Tax Law: The Essentials

1.1 Introduction

Polish tax law has undergone a lengthy process of evolution which has coincided with a number of fundamental political, systemic, economic, and social shifts. All these shifts have directly influenced the shape of contemporary Polish tax law as well as setting the strategic directions of its development. The turbulent history of Poland saw events that altered dramatically not only tax law proper but also the functions assigned to public levies.

The current status of Polish tax law was mainly influenced by the changes of the early 1990s. This was when the central and local self-government systems were established. Both these systems of administration have their own powers, budgets, and own income that covers for their expenditure. Of course, taxes play a very important role in their budgets. The units of local self-government at all levels (*gmina* – municipality, *powiat* – district, and *województwo* – voivodeship or province) are also public law bodies authorised to collect taxes. The period of political and economic transformation referred to above also marked the beginning of a major tax law reform. The taxation system of the communist era was subject to revision and gradually supplanted by an approach pursued in free market economies. Also, some new solutions were adopted not seen in the tax law of communist Poland. They primarily governed the taxation of income (personal income tax and corporate income tax) and economic transactions (tax on goods and services). Poland's entry into the European Union (EU) necessitated a profound adjustment of Polish tax law to the EU standards. At the same time, today's tax law has preserved some regulations that were created back in the former political system. For example, the tax on land of agricultural holdings (agricultural tax), inheritance and gift tax. Consequently, today's Polish tax law is a mixture of EU solutions and domestic regulations derived from the Polish fiscal tradition. Undoubtedly, it is also a fast-growing scholarly discipline addressed extensively across all the major research centres Poland-wide. At universities, tax law is part of the core curriculum of not only law but also of administration, economics, or management programmes.

1.2 The Concept and Structure of Tax

The Polish tax system failed to provide a legal (statutory) definition of tax for a relatively long period. This gap was filled by the academia which proposed a theoretical definition of tax. It says that tax is a cash benefit to a body governed by public law (state or local self-government), determined unilaterally by that body and having a general, essential, non-returnable, non-reciprocal, and compulsory nature.

No earlier than in 1997 was the Tax Ordinance Act adopted which provided a statutory definition of tax by incorporating the elements of the scholarly definition.[1] According to the Tax Ordinance Act, tax is **a public, non-reciprocal, compulsory and non-refundable pecuniary performance in favour of the State Treasury, voivodeship, district, or municipal budget.**

Non-reciprocal character of tax means that the taxpayer paying tax should not expect anything in return (any benefit) from the state or a self-government unit. This differentiates taxes from fees or charges that are paid in exchange for some administrative service or formal service, e.g. issuing an identification document. Consequently, the taxpayer may not claim anything from the state or local self-government based on the principle of reciprocity.

Tax is a **compulsory** contribution. This means that it can be collected by force, i.e. through administrative enforcement.

A characteristic feature of tax is that it is **non-refundable**, which means that any tax collected legally is not to be returned. This, of course, does not apply to a tax overpayment which is subject to refund.

Tax is a pecuniary performance. This means that, in principle, it is collected **in cash,** although the law also provides for the seizure of taxpayer's assets if tax arrears occur.

Besides the attributed named above, each tax also has its own unique structure. It consists of several elements specific to the type of tax. These are: 1) taxable person; 2) taxable object; 3) tax base; 4) tax scale; 5) exemptions and reliefs.

---

1   Article 6 of the Act of 29 August 1997 – Tax Ordinance (consolidated text: Journal of Laws of 2018, item 800 as amended), hereafter "the Tax Ordinance" or "the TOA."

There are two types of taxable persons (or tax subjects). **Taxable persons** are both ones that impose and collect tax for themselves (the state and local self-government) and ones that are obliged to pay tax, i.e. **the taxpayer.**

The taxpayer is not the same as the tax remitter. **Tax remitter** is an intermediary between the state and the taxpayer. The tax remitter's obligations are threefold: 1) to calculate tax; 2) to collect tax from the taxpayer; 3) to pay the tax to the tax authority within a prescribed time limit. In Poland, the institution of tax remitter occurs both in taxes collected for the state budget and those feeding the local self-government budgets. When collecting some of the local taxes, (e.g. agricultural tax, forest tax), there is an option of paying the tax through another entity – the tax collector. **Tax collector** performs the same activities as the remitter, but it does not calculate the tax since it is fixed by the relevant tax authority. The tax collector only collects the tax and forwards it to the relevant tax authority.

Taxable object is a taxable item or fact/phenomenon. Knowing the object of taxation means knowing what the tax is levied on.

Tax base is the concretisation of the object of taxation. The tax base is subject to a tax rate expressed as an amount or percentage value. The rates in a given tax make **a tax scale.** Typically, there are two types of tax scales: 1) proportional; 2) non-proportional (progressive).

The **proportional scale** has a fixed tax rate. This means that despite the changing tax base the rate is always the same, and the amount of levy varies in proportion to the changing value of the tax base. The **non-proportional (progressive) scale** has a varied rate depending on the size of the tax base.

1.3 Classification of Taxes

The doctrine of Polish tax law classifies taxes based on a number of criteria. As a result, not only does a uniform classification system not exist, there is even no uniform tax nomenclature following such a division. In addition, the existing taxes often reveal a differentiated internal structure, which makes them – even when applying a uniform tax classification methodology – exhibit characteristics specific to different types of taxation. This leads to fundamental differences in the assessment of the nature of a given tax, and this is not a mere theoretical dispute. The proper assessment of the nature of tax (e.g. property or income tax) has an impact on the approach to and the result of interpretation of the relevant regulations applicable in practice by, e.g. administrative courts. The tax classification given below does not exhaust the entire subject of taxation and covers only the most common of its forms.

The basic criterion for the classification of taxes is the type of public entity which benefits from the tax proceeds. Bearing that in mind, we have the following types of taxes:

a) state taxes – supplying the state budget, such as income taxes, value-added tax (VAT), excise tax, gambling tax.
b) local government (municipal) taxes – supplying the local budgets, such as real property tax, agricultural tax, forest tax, inheritance and gift tax, tax on civil law transaction. The choice of this tax division criterion adopted as fundamental for this study does not mean that the other criteria are of minor or secondary importance.

So, the following taxes can be distinguished based on the method of calculation:

a) indirect: the legal concept of such taxes allows for a mechanism of incorporating their value in the price of a service or goods offered; this value is shown on an invoice (VAT, excise tax).
b) direct: their legal concept does not allow for a mechanism of incorporating the value of tax in the price of a service or goods offered (income taxes, inheritance and gift tax, agricultural tax).

With regard to the source of tax, it can be divided into two main groups:

a) income taxes: imposed on the taxpayer's income.
b) taxes on wealth: imposed on the taxpayer's assets or property.

In addition, there is an option of taxing the taxpayer's income upon its disbursement, i.e. its consumption. Such taxes are known as consumption taxes.

Irrespective of this classification, a number of other theoretical types of taxes are given in the Polish literature on the subject, e.g. revenue tax, income and revenue tax, turnover tax, or wealth and revenue tax.

1.4 The Sources and Principles of Drafting Tax Law

The sources of Polish tax law include: the Constitution of the Republic of Poland, parliamentary acts, ratified international agreements, regulations, and acts of local law.

The Constitution of the Republic of Poland is the supreme act of Polish law, including tax law. It contains some general rules that must be observed both when drafting and applying tax law. The Constitution defines the legal basis of taxation, some elements of tax structure, the procedure for enacting tax laws as well as the powers of self-government bodies to make tax regulations. According to the Constitution, everyone should comply with the responsibilities and public duties, including the payment of taxes, as specified by statute. In parallel, the Constitution explicitly provides that the imposition of taxes, as well as other public imposts, the specification of taxable persons and the rates of taxation, as well as the principles for granting tax reliefs and remissions, along with categories of taxpayers exempt from taxation, is done by the means of statute. This principle corresponds to the standards of modern legislations and reaffirms the statute as the **exclusive** instrument governing the imposition of taxes and other public levies. Thus, the Constitution defines another and no less important source of Polish tax law – the statute.

Another source of tax law is ratified international agreements. After publication, such agreements become an integral part of the national legal system. They take precedence of application over statutes in the event of conflicting provisions. Among these, double taxation agreements are particularly noteworthy. Independently of the international instruments, after the Polish accession to the European Union, the EU legal standards attained a special status among the sources of tax law. In principle, the application of EU law prevails over national law.

Another source of Polish tax law are regulations. They are issued by the bodies named in the Constitution, pursuant to a specific mandate contained in statute. They have a role of implementing measures. Regulations cannot amend or modify the content of the Constitution or statutes. The bodies authorised to issue regulations are the President of the Republic of Poland, the Council of Ministers, the Prime Minister, and ministers.

Another source of tax law is the acts of local law. According to the Constitution, the units of local self-government are empowered to determine the level of local taxes and fees within the limit specified by statute. Local self-government bodies, based on and within the limit of competence given in statute, enact local laws that are in force in the territory administered by these bodies. The rules and procedures of making such acts are prescribed by a specific statute. The acts of local law may specify the rights and obligations of entities indicated therein; still their territorial scope is limited to the area administered by the law-making bodies. In the light of the Constitution, the acts of local law cannot, of itself, impose additional fiscal burdens on a given territory. A tax liability can only be imposed by statute. It should be stressed that this rule is not prejudiced by the institution of the so-called self-taxation of the municipality residents for public purposes. Any imposition of additional tax should be preceded by a local referendum. The legal basis and course of the procedure are prescribed in a separate statute.

In the Polish legal system, judicial decisions are not regarded as a source of tax law. Courts of law do not have the power to make laws. Their judgements are binding only in particular cases. However, there is no doubt that they enjoy a high status in the practice of interpretation of tax law.

The enactment of tax law is governed by specific rules (standards) supplied by the doctrine (science) of tax law and by case law. To some extent, these rules curtail the parliament's freedom to impose fiscal burdens. The most noteworthy of them are:

1) the principle of non-retroactivity (*lex retro non agit*);
2) the principle of tax justice;
3) the principle of equality and universality of taxation;
4) the principle of acquired rights;
5) the principle of adjustment period (*vacatio legis*).

The principle of the law not acting retroactively *(lex retro non agit)* means that no regulation can be laid down that would require the application of the newly established standards to acts or events that had occurred before that regulation entered into force.

Both the science of tax law and case law assume that the state should seek tax justice by distributing the fiscal burden in accordance with the principles of equality and universality. This, in turn, implies the obligation of aligning the taxation process with the constitutional principles of equality and social justice. What follows, taxpayers who are in the same position should be treated equally, i.e. without discrimination against or in favour of them. Still, some statutory exceptions to the principle of universality of taxation are not excluded.

According to the principle of protection of acquired rights, protected are both the rights acquired through a specific act of law and the rights acquired under the general terms, i.e. by statute. This principle does not apply to rights acquired in a foul or unfair manner.

The requirement of *vacatio legis* is primarily about maintaining a period between the formal enactment of a law and its coming into force. In principle, the minimum period of *vacatio legis* is 14 days. In the case of statutes introducing changes to the personal income tax, the publication of the amended law should take place no later than one month before the end of the fiscal year. This entails (i) a prohibition of introducing changes to taxes settled in the annual period during the fiscal year and (ii) the requirement to lay down the so-called transitional provisions that aim to assist the entities affected by the amended law in adapting to the new or modified obligations.

2 Tax Obligations

2.1 When a Tax Obligation Arises

The key concepts in Polish tax law – without them any further dispute and study of fiscal law is next to impossible – are tax liability and tax obligation. Both these notions have been defined in the Tax Ordinance Act (TOA). In addition to the occurrence, expiration, security, and responsibility for tax obligations, the act also regulates the operation and competence of tax authorities; agreements on transaction prices; tax proceedings; investigation activities; tax inspection; fiscal secrecy; exchange of tax information with other states, and penal measures.

For the sake of further discussion, it is necessary to define the concept of tax liability. The TOA reads as follows, "an unspecified duty, resulting from the fiscal laws, to bear a compulsory pecuniary performance in relation to the occurrence of an event specified by such laws." It should be emphasised that the Polish doctrine of tax law takes a double approach to the nature of tax liability. On the one hand, this liability is an abstract duty arising at the time of occurrence of a fact under tax law; this fact has been identified in the hypothesis of the tax law standard, independently of the will of those subject to that liability. On the other hand, the authors also emphasise the concretisation of the abstract duty manifesting itself in that a given entity – through its specific conduct defined by the legal standard – falls within the scope of tax liability. In addition, the Polish literature on the subject also highlights some extra elements that make up the concept of tax liability. These are material (pecuniary performance) and procedural liabilities (an obligation to register a taxpayer, submit a tax form, or fiscal record-keeping).

The materialisation, or a specific consequence, of tax liability is tax obligation. In other words, every tax obligation is a consequence of prior tax liability. Still, tax liability does no always become tax obligation. This may be due, for example, to the limitation of the right to assessment (to be discussed below) or the application of a specific exemption. The TOA defines tax obligation as "an obligation of the taxpayer, resulting from tax liability, to pay a tax in favour of the State Treasury, voivodeship, district or municipality in the amount, within the time limit and in the place determined in the provisions of tax law." Thus, the basis of a tax obligation is a relation under tax law between an entity (debtor) and a tax authority representing the State Treasury or a unit of the local self-government (creditor). The idea of this relation is that it arises under statute and not by an agreement in the first place. Second, the consequence of the occurrence of an obligation under statute is the lack of freedom in shaping the extent of this obligation. Third, the creditor in such a relation is, in principle, a body governed by public law, so any equality of the parties is excluded, unlike in the relations (and obligations) formed under civil law. In addition, in the pecuniary sense, the object of tax liability is not only a tax but also tax advances, tax instalments, as well as tax arrears and the related delay interest.

Polish tax law points to two ways in which a tax obligation may arise.

First, a tax obligation may arise *ex lege*, that is, **upon the occurrence of an event related to the rise of such an obligation according to statute.** When this method comes into play, the taxpayer should be aware of the relevant tax regulations and follow them correctly, since they are obliged to calculate the amount of tax and effect the timely payment to the competent tax authority. The role of the tax authority is only that of verifying the correctness of the taxpayer's performance of the tax obligation, for example, in the course of investigation activities or tax inspections. If the tax authority finds that the taxpayer has failed to pay the tax in full or in part, has failed to submit a tax return or that the amount of tax obligation is different from that shown in the return or is absent from the return, it determines the proper amount of the tax obligation. This decision is aimed only to determine the existence of the obligation, hence its name, "determination decision." In principle, *ex lege* tax liabilities arise, but not only, in such taxes as: personal income tax, corporate income tax, value-added tax (VAT), excise tax, tax on transactions under civil law, tax on the means of transport, and in connection with legal persons and entities without legal personality: real property tax, agricultural tax, and forest tax.

The other way in which a tax obligation may arise in **upon the date of service of the tax authority's decision providing the amount of the obligation.** In this case, the taxpayer receives a constitutive decision from the tax authority, that is, one that clarifies the amount, deadline, and place of payment of the tax. This way is very convenient to the taxpayer as their responsibility is limited only to the payment of tax without having to calculate it beforehand. However, the above method makes the tax collection process more expensive, which seems to be at variance with the principle of cost-effectiveness of taxation. The emergence of a tax obligation at the time of service of the decision with its amount is seen in such taxes as: inheritance and gift tax (unless the tax is collected by the tax remitter), personal income tax (levied on persons receiving income from undisclosed sources), or real property tax, agricultural tax, or forest tax (levied on natural persons).[2]

The provisions of Polish law require that the tax authority issue a decision with the amount of tax obligation within a specific time limit. The rule is that the tax decision should be served to the taxpayer within three years – beginning with the end of the calendar year in which the tax obligation arises. Otherwise, the right to assess the tax obligation will expire. As a result, the taxpayer will not pay the tax for the given fiscal year. The three-year period may be extended to five years beginning with the end of the calendar year in which the tax obligation arises if the taxpayer:

- has failed to submit a tax return within the time limit stipulated in tax law or;
- has not disclosed in the submitted tax return all the data necessary to determine the amount of tax obligation.

In specific cases, the said time limit may be suspended but for not longer than two years. This happens where the issuing of a decision is contingent upon the settlement of a preliminary issue by another authority or court.[3]

---

2 More about discharging tax obligations: R. Mastalski, *Prawo podatkowe*, C.H. Beck, Warsaw 2017a, pp. 214–221; H. Dzwonkowski, "*Powstawanie obowiązku, wymiar i wykonywanie zobowiązań oraz roszczeń wynikających ze stosunków prawno podatkowych*," [in:] *Prawo podatkowe*, ed. H. Dzwonkowski, C.H. Beck, Warsaw 2012, pp. 118–130; J. Małecki, "*Zobowiązania podatkowe w świetle Ordynacji podatkowej*," [in:] *Podatki i prawo podatkowe*, eds. A. Gomułowicz, J. Małecki, LexisNexis, Warsaw 2010c, pp. 380–386; M. Szustek-Janowska, "*Zobowiązania podatkowe*," [in:] *Prawo podatkowe-część ogólna i szczegółowa*, ed. W. Wójtowicz, C.H. Beck, Warsaw 2009, pp. 32–37.
3 H. Dzwonkowski, "Powstanie obowiązku podatkowego i przedawnienie prawa wymiaru zobowiązania," *Prawo i Podatki* 2009, No. 8, p. 19 et seq.

2.2 Securing the Performance of Tax Obligations

2.2.1 Securing Tax Obligations before Payment Deadline

The main purpose of the institution of securing the performance of tax obligations is the safeguarding of the interest of the tax creditor by ensuring that a given tax obligation is paid (or settled) in the future. The performance of a tax obligation is secured before the payment deadline if there is a well-founded fear that it is not met. As naturally follows, the security of performance can be ensured only for those obligations whose payment deadlines have not yet expired. The TOA contains an open-end list of conditions that must be met in order to take advantage of the said security measure. These conditions allude to situations in which the taxpayer fails to pay their public levies on a permanent basis or disposes of their property to hinder or frustrate the enforcement procedure. The obligation is secured on the taxpayer's or taxpayer and their spouse's property.

The other option of securing the performance of a tax obligation may be in the course of tax proceedings, tax inspection or customs, and fiscal inspection, before issuing the decision: establishing the amount of tax obligation (relative to the obligations arising upon the service of the decision); determining the amount of the obligation (relative to the obligations arising *ex lege*); determining the amount of a tax refund (issued in relation to VAT). The tax authority, on the basis of the information available on the amount of the taxable base, issues a decision on security to determine: (i) the approximate amount of the tax obligation, in case the security is set up before issuing the decision establishing the amount of tax obligation; or (ii) the approximate amount of tax obligation and the amount of delay interest due on the day of issuing the decision, in case the security is set up before issuing the decision determining the amount of tax obligation.

The performance of tax obligations can be secured not only on the taxpayer's property, but also on the tax remitter, tax collector, and other third parties' property (e.g. partners in partnerships, members of the management of companies or other legal persons, such as cooperatives, foundations, or associations).

The decision on security expires:

– 14 days after the service of the decision establishing the amount of tax obligation;
– on the day of service of the decision determining the amount of tax obligation;
– on the day of service of the decision determining the amount of a tax refund.

The security of performance of the decision may be ensured at the request of the taxpayer (tax remitter, tax collector, or selected third parties) or according to the provisions on the administrative enforcement. The rule is that the requested security is given priority over the security pursued under the provisions of the administrative enforcement. On the other hand, where the request for security is submitted after the establishment of the security under the administrative enforcement, the scope of the security established under the said enforcement is revoked or amended. Securing the performance of the decision at the taxpayer's (tax remitter, tax collector, or selected third parties) request is carried out by the tax authority accepting the security indicated in the request in one of the following forms: a bank or insurance guarantee; a bank suretyship; a bill of exchange guaranteed by a bank; a cheque guaranteed by a domestic bank of the cheque drawer; a registered pledge on securities issued by the State Treasury or National Bank of Poland according to their nominal value; crediting the tax authority's deposit account; a written, irrevocable authorisation of the tax authority, confirmed by a bank or a co-operative credit-saving fund, to exclusively dispose of funds accumulated on a time deposit.

If they taxpayer fails to submit a request indicating the preferred form of security, the tax authority ensures the security through the administrative enforcement procedure which can cover: the seizure of money, salary, receivables from bank accounts, other receivables, property rights or movables; establishment of a compulsory mortgage on property; creation of a pledge on a seagoing vessel or a seagoing vessel under construction with registration in the naval register (compulsory ship mortgage); prohibition on the sale and encumbrance of a property without the land register or whose land register has been damaged or lost; prohibition on the sale of the cooperative member's right to residential premises, cooperative member's right to commercial premises or the right to a detached house in a housing cooperative.[4]

2.2.2 Compulsory Mortgage

The idea of compulsory mortgage in Polish tax law is that, unlike in a standard mortgage where the owner of a property enters into a voluntary agreement with the creditor, it is set up without the property owner's consent. Oftentimes, such a mortgage is established against the owner's will.

The institution of compulsory mortgage can be used by the State Treasury and the local self-government. It is set up to secure tax obligations that arise upon service of the decision establishing the amount of tax obligation (the deadline for the payment of tax by the taxpayer has not yet expired) as well as tax arrears and delay interest on these arrears. Compulsory mortgages can also be established on receivables due from the tax remitter, tax collector, legal successor, or a third party.

In principle, a compulsory mortgage may be established on a real property or fractional part of a real property, provided that it is the taxpayer's share; a real property that is the joint co-ownership of the taxpayer and his or her spouse; a real property that is the joint co-ownership of the partners in a civil law partnership, or a fractional part of the title to a real property that is a share in a civil law partnership – due to the partnership's tax arrears. Besides, a compulsory mortgage may also be established on the rights related to property, such as perpetual usufruct, as well as on receivables secured by mortgage, or a seagoing vessel or a vessel under construction entered in to the naval register.

A compulsory mortgage is established by making an entry in the land register. It is made at the request of the tax authority by the competent district court and by the competent maritime chamber in the case of a ship mortgage.

---

4 More: W. Stachurski, "*Zabezpieczenie wykonania zobowiązań podatkowych*," [in:] *Ordynacja podatkowa. Komentarz*, ed. L. Etel, Wolters Kluwer, Warsaw 2017, pp. 408–436.

The rule is that tax obligations secured by a mortgage are not subject to limitation.[5]

2.2.3 Treasury Lien

Treasury lien is an institution that the State Treasury and local self-government units may employ in order to secure tax obligations arising upon service of the decision establishing the amount of tax obligation (the deadline for the payment of tax by the taxpayer has not yet expired) as well as tax arrears and delay interest on these arrears. While in the case of a mortgage which applies to real property and property rights, the treasury lien applies to movable property and transferable property rights owned or co-owned by the taxpayer. A prerequisite for a treasury lien to be established is that the value of particular items or rights on the date of the pledge be at least PLN 12,400. In addition, a treasury lien may also be established on receivables from tax remitters, tax payers, legal successors, or third parties responsible for tax arrears.

A treasury lien arises on the day of entry into the register of treasury liens kept by the heads of tax offices. A treasury lien is made pursuant to the served decision (i) establishing the amount of the tax obligation; (ii) determining the amount of the tax obligation; (iii) determining the amount of delay interest; (iv) determining the amount of a tax refund; (v) on the tax liability of a tax remitter, tax collector, third party, or inheritor. A treasury lien expires by force of law when the tax obligation expires or when the entry in treasury lien register is deleted, or on a day of an enforcement sale of the subject of the lien.[6]

---

5 R. Mastalski, "*Zabezpieczenie wykonania zobowiązań podatkowych*," [in:] *Ordynacja podatkowa. Komentarz*, eds. B. Adamiak, J. Borkowski, P. Borszowski, R. Mastalski, J. Zubrzycki, Unimex, Wrocław 2017c, pp. 310–322.

6 H. Dzwonkowski, J. Kondratowska, "*Zabezpieczenie wykonania zobowiązań podatkowych*," [in:] *Ordynacja podatkowa. Komentarz*, C.H. Beck, Warsaw 2016, pp. 378–388.

2.3 Expiry of Tax Obligations

2.3.1 Introduction

Polish tax law provides for two methods of expiry of a tax obligation. The first method is most desirable from the viewpoint of the fiscal interests of the state or a local self-government unit. In this approach, the expiry of a tax obligations coincides with the satisfaction of the tax creditor. The effective methods of expiry of tax obligations are:

- payment of tax;
- collection of tax by a tax remitter or tax collector;
- deduction;
- transfer of ownership of things or property rights;
- crediting an overpayment or tax refund;
- seizing real property or property rights in enforcement proceedings;
- acquisition of the entire inheritance by the State Treasury or a unit of local self-government confirmed by a legally binding decision on acquisition of inheritance – taking effect on the date of the opening of the inheritance.

In the other method, the expiry of a tax obligations does not entail the satisfaction of the tax creditor. The ineffective methods of expiry of tax obligations are:

- limitation of the period of obligation;
- waving a tax collection;
- remission of tax arrears;
- exemption as a result of an interpretation.

2.3.2 Effective Expiry of Tax Obligations

2.3.2.1 *Payment*

Payment of tax is the basic method of satisfying tax obligations. The tax payment deadlines are provided in the provisions of individual tax laws. This is typically true of obligations that arise *ex lege*. On the other hand, in the case of tax obligations that arise upon service of the decision, the deadline for payment of tax is 14 days from the date of service of the decision establishing the amount of a tax obligation. Still, it should be stressed that in certain Polish taxes in which the tax obligation arises upon service of the decision, the relevant provisions of the law may also specify payment dates in the calendar. This is the case, for example, in real property tax, agricultural tax, or forest tax. If, therefore, in the levies referred to above the decision establishing the amount of the tax obligation was not served at least 14 days before the deadline of payment of tax, the first tax advance or the first tax instalment, then the payment deadline is 14 days from the date of service of the decision establishing the amount of the tax obligation.

Payment of tax can be a cash or non-cash operation. In the case of cash payment, the payment day is the day of paying the tax, whereas in the non-cash payment, the payment day is the day of debiting the taxpayer's bank account. However, it must be emphasised that business entities that are required to maintain accounts or a revenue and expense book are obliged to pay tax by credit transfer. The exception to this rule is the payment of stamp duty which can be made in cash. Moreover, cash payments can be effected by micro-enterprises, i.e. entities that (i) have employed fewer than ten employees over one of the last two fiscal years; (ii) have generated an annual net revenue on the sale of goods and services and on financial operation not exceeding the equivalent of EUR 2 million; or (iii) the total assets in its balance sheet at the end of one of the last two fiscal years have not exceeded the equivalent of EUR 2 million. Taxpayers conducting an economic activity who pay taxes not related to their activity are also released from the obligation to pay tax via a credit transfer. In addition, tax may be paid in cash when it is collected by tax remitters or tax collectors, and also when the payment of tax, in accordance with tax law, is made with securities or excise stamps.[7]

Until the end of 2015, only the taxpayer had been able to pay due tax, and the payment by any other entity, e.g. a member of the family, had been ineffective and had not caused the expiry of the tax obligation. Beginning with 1 January 2016, this rule was relaxed for practical reasons. The amendment allowed that, besides the taxpayer, the due tax can also be paid by their spouse, descendant, ascendant, stepson, siblings, stepfather, and stepmother. If the tax is secured by a compulsory mortgage or treasury

---

7   B. Brzeziński, *Prawo podatkowe*, Dom Organizatora, Toruń 2000a, pp. 96–99.

lien, it can be paid by the current holder of the mortgaged or pledged item. On the other hand, if the amount of tax does not exceed PLN 1,000, taxpayer's levy may be paid by another entity, e.g. partner in a partnership or a contractor.

If a tax is not paid on time, then turns tax arrears. Tax arrears are also overdue tax advances or instalments. A consequence of delaying the payment of tax on time is delay interest. As a rule, the taxpayer calculates delay interest on their own, but, in some circumstances, it may also be the tax remitter, tax collector, legal successor, or a third party. Interest is accrued from the day following the date of payment deadline or the date on which the tax remitter or tax collector are obliged to make the payment of tax to the tax authority's bank account.

The rate of interest on overdue payments is equal to 200% of the base interest rate of the Lombard credit facility, in accordance with the regulations on the National Bank of Poland, and 2%. However, the provisions of tax law provide that the interest rate cannot be less than 8%. Still, it should be emphasised that, in certain circumstances, it is possible to apply a reduced interest rate on delayed payments. If so, it amounts to 50% of the base rate. To ensure that this rate is applied, the taxpayer must submit a legally effective corrected tax return no later than within six months after the deadline for submitting the return. In addition, the payment of tax arrears must take place within seven days from the date of submitting the corrected tax return. In contrast, the taxpayer will not be entitled to a reduced interest rate for overdue payment if a corrected tax return has been submitted in response to the notification of an impending tax inspection.

Due to the frequent taxpayers' fraudulent behaviour in indirect taxes, which seriously depletes the revenues to the state budget, an increased interest on arrears has been introduced. It amounts to 150% of the base rate of delay interest and applies to arrears in goods and services tax and in excise tax. Under binding tax law, the increased rate of delay interest is applicable when, in the course of action taken by a tax authority (e.g. tax proceedings, tax inspection), the tax authority discloses the taxpayer's failure to submit a tax return despite the existing obligation to do so. In addition, the increased rate applies when the amount of tax obligation has been lowered or the amount of overpayment or tax refund has been raised and such fraudulent behaviour has been revealed in the course of investigation by the tax authority (tax proceedings or tax inspection). The higher rate of interest for overdue payment is also effective when the taxpayer has corrected the tax return as a result of action taken by the tax authority, provided that the difference between the amount of tax due and the amount declared by the taxpayer exceeds 25% and is higher than five times the minimum wage.

Under existing tax law, in certain circumstances, the taxpayer may have recourse to a **relief in the repayment of their obligations.** At the request of the taxpayer, the authority, in cases justified by a taxpayer's valid interest or public interest, may defer the date of payment of tax or agree to payment in instalments. On the other hand, if the taxpayer delays the payment of tax, the arrears with due delay interest may be deferred or rearranged into instalments. Where a taxpayer conducts an economic activity, then the tax authority is obliged to investigate whether the awarded tax relief is not in conflict with the regulations governing public aid and *de minimis* aid. The decision to award the relief in question is discretionary. Even if it the tax authority finds that there is an "important taxpayer's interest" or "important public interest" coming into play, it may refuse to award the requested relief. The right to request a relief in the repayment of tax obligations is also vested with the tax remitters, tax collectors, successors, and third parties. The award of the relief in the repayment of tax obligations representing income to the state budget entails an **extension fee** setup by the tax authority based on the amount of tax or tax arrears. The extension fee is equal to the reduced rate of interest for overdue payment. However, this fee is not applicable when the reason for issuing the decision on a tax relief is a natural disaster or mishap. In addition, the tax authority may refrain from imposing an extension fee if the decision is related to the ongoing arrangement proceedings. In the case of taxes feeding the municipal budget, the municipal council may, by way of a resolution, introduce an extension fee.

2.3.2.2 Deduction of Claims

A tax obligation may also expire as a result of a deduction. Deduction is an institution borrowed into tax law from civil law. If two entities are both a debtor and a creditor to one another, they can perform a set-off of mutual obligations. Under tax law, deduction can be employed both to tax obligations and tax arrears including interest. A request for deduction can be made by a taxpayer who is a debtor (tax debtor) and a creditor to the State Treasury (entitled to specific receivables). If such a request is submitted, the deduction day is the day of filing the request. Deductions may also be made *ex officio*. This being the case, the deduction day is the day in which the tax authority issues the decision approving deduction. To take advantage of this institution, the taxpayer's claim must be mutual, undisputed, and due. The list of claims subject to a deduction is closed and has a compensatory nature. The listed claims are, among others: the acquisition of real property by the State Treasury for the purpose of justifying its expropriation or the expropriation of real property; compensation awarded in the decision of a government administrative body; compensation for an unjust conviction, provisional custody or detention; final court judgement or settlement to compensate for harm resulting from a decision of a government administrative body.[8]

A deduction can also apply to a mutual, undisputed and due taxpayer's claim to state budgetary units by virtue of public procurement resulting from agreements concluded under the provisions on public procurement. In Poland, the budgetary units are the organisational units of the public finance sector, having no legal personality. Their expenditures are the expenditures of the state budget or local self-government budget and their revenues are the revenues of the state budget or local self-government (e.g. offices, schools).

A deduction may also be applied to the tax obligations or tax arrears that constitute a municipal revenue. In this case, however, the list of claims for a deduction is narrower. It fails to include, for example, compensation for an unjust conviction, provisional custody or detention.

2.3.2.3 Transfer of Ownership of Things or Property Rights

A tax obligation may also expire through the transfer by the taxpayer to the State Treasury (in taxes feeding the state revenue) or the municipality (in taxes feeding the municipal revenue) of ownership of things or property rights. This way of expiring a tax obligation is applicable only to tax

---

8   More: H. Dzwonkowski, M. Kurzac, "*Wygaśnięcie zobowiązań podatkowych*", [in:] *Ordynacja podatkowa. Komentarz*, ed. H. Dzwonkowski, C.H. Beck, Warsaw 2016, pp. 451–457.

arrears.[9] This measure is employed upon the taxpayer's request. In the case of taxes that feed the state budget, the transfer of ownership of things or property rights is carried out under an agreement concluded with the taxpayer and an entity representing the State Treasury (*starosta* – district head) following the consent of the head of the tax office. Only after the agreement has been concluded, the head of the tax office decides to close the obligation.

When it comes to taxes feeding the municipal budget, the relevant agreement is entered into between the taxpayer and the mayor.

2.3.2.4 Overpayment

In the Polish tax system, the following amounts are regarded as overpayment:

- overpaid or unduly paid tax;
- tax collected by a tax remitter unduly or in an amount higher than the amount due;
- an obligation paid by a tax remitter or tax collector, if in the decision concerning the liability of tax remitter or tax collector, it was determined unduly or in an amount higher than the amount due;
- an obligation paid by a third party or successor if, in the decision on their tax liability or in the decision establishing the amount of tax obligation of the deceased, it was determined unduly or in an amount higher than the amount due.

Tax law specifies two situations when an overpayment arises. **First,** an overpayment arises (i) as of the day when the taxpayer pays tax that is undue or is in a higher amount than due or, when tax is collected by the tax remitter; or (ii) on the day of collection of undue tax or in a higher amount than due. With regard to other entities, such as a third party or successor, the amount of overpayment arises (i) on the day of payment if the amount due was determined unduly or in amount higher than the amount due and, in the case of the tax remitter or tax collector; or (ii) on the day of payment of tax in the amount higher than the amount collected. **Second,** an overpayment may arise as from the date of submitting a tax statement or

---

9   Z. Ofiarski, *Ogólne prawo podatkowe. Zagadnienia materialnoprawne i proceduralne*, Lexis Nexis, Warsaw 2010, pp. 145–147.

tax return. It should be emphasised that the overlapping occurrence of an overpayment and the submission of a tax statement or tax return has been limited to income taxes, hydrocarbon tax, excise tax, and payments from profits for the fiscal year by the sole-shareholder companies of the State Treasury and state-owned enterprises.

If the time of an overpayment arising is the same as the time of submitting a tax statement, the determination of the amount of the overpayment is done based on the tax statement delivered by the taxpayer. In all other cases, the amount of overpayment, except where it has arisen from a judgement of the Constitutional Tribunal or of the Court of Justice of the European Union, is determined in a decision of the tax authority.

As follows from the general rule, an overpayment along with its interest reduce *ex officio* the amount of tax arrears including delay interest, delay interest on late tax advances, reminder costs, and current tax obligations. In the absence of the above amounts due, the overpayment with interest is returned *ex officio* unless the taxpayer submits an application for the overpayment to be credited, in whole or in part, to future fiscal obligations. As a rule, the deadline for the return of an overpayment is three months from the date of submitting the tax statement or tax return or 30 days from the date of the decision or entry into force of the judgement of the Constitutional Tribunal or publication of the judgement of the Court of Justice of the European Union in the *Official Journal of the European Union.*

Overpayments are interest-bearing at the rate equal to delay interest on tax arrears. An overpayment bears interest until the day of refund or, alternatively, crediting it to the overdue or current tax obligations or until the date of submission of the application requesting that the overpayment to be credited to future tax obligations.

The right to refund of an overpayment expires five years after the end of the calendar year in which its refund date expired.[10]

---

10 More about overpayment: B. Brzeziński, H. Filipczyk, "*Nadpłata,*" [in:] *Nowelizacja Ordynacji podatkowej*, eds. B. Brzeziński, W. Morawski, Wolters Kluwer, Warsaw 2016, p. 109 et seq.

2.3.3 Ineffective Expiry of Tax Obligations

2.3.3.1 Remission of Tax Arrears

An ineffective method of expiry of a tax obligation is the remission of the tax arrears in whole or in part. Remission can be decided by a tax authority which can also cancel delay interests or an extension fee. A taxpayer intending to take advantage of this method is obliged to submit an application indicating the existence of at least one of the two prerequisites, namely an "important public interest" or "important taxpayer's interest." It should be emphasised that the occurrence of one of the above conditions does not oblige the tax authority to remit any arrears. The tax authority if free to decide both ways and the award of this tax preference is discretionary. In this context, it is advisable to explain what is meant by "important public interest" and "important taxpayer's interest" since the TOA uses the wording a number of times (e.g. on the waiver of tax collection, deferral of tax payment, allowing tax or tax arrears to be paid in instalments or in the release of the tax remitter from the obligation to collect tax from the taxpayers). It should be noted that none of these concepts has been defined by the legislator, thus leaving the interpretation to the tax authorities. Based on the judicial and administrative case law, it can be inferred that an "important taxpayer's interest" occurs when the taxpayer is in a difficult life situation which can even threaten his or her life. Equally important is to ascertain that, as a result of the taxpayer's poor financial position, their solvency has deteriorated, thus rendering the fulfilment of their tax obligation impossible. On the other hand, an "important public interest" occurs when it is proven to be connected with the obligation to respect the values shared by the whole society, such as: justice, security, equality, citizens' confidence in public authorities, or the efficiency of the state apparatus.

Third parties and the successors of the taxpayer and tax remitter may also apply for the remission of tax arrears. It should be underlined that the remission of tax arrears also entails the cancellation of delay interest in whole or in such a part in which the tax arrears have been remitted. Where a taxpayer conducts an economic activity, the tax authority may, at the taxpayer's request, remit tax arrears which (i) is not a public aid; (ii) is a *de minimis* aid; or (iii) is a public aid, extended, for example, to repair damages caused by natural disasters, prevent or eliminate serious cross-sectoral disruptions to the state economy, or to support domestic entrepreneurs involved in a business undertaking pursued in European interest.

It should be emphasised that, in certain circumstances, the tax authorities may remit tax arrears *ex officio*. Polish law provides for a limited list of cases in which this procedure is possible. However, they all come down to the situation in which the taxpayer's assets are insufficient to satisfy the tax obligation or where the taxpayer dies and leaves no assets or successors.[11]

2.3.3.2 Limitation Period of Obligation

Limitation is among the ineffective methods of expiry of tax obligations. In Polish tax law, tax obligations are subject to limitation after five years from the end of the calendar year in which the tax payment deadline expired. However, under certain conditions, this time limit may be suspended. This can happen as a result of: lodging a claim to an administrative court against the decision concerning such an obligation; initiating proceedings in matters of a revenue offence or a revenue petty offence, provided that the suspicion of the offence or petty offence is linked to the non-performance of the obligation; filing a declaratory action to the common court to establish the existence or non-existence of a legal relationship or right; if the possibility of establishing or determining the tax obligation results from double taxation treaties or other ratified treaties; or requesting the desired information from a tax authority of another state.

In addition, Polish tax law stipulates that the limitation period may be interrupted as a result of performing an action provided for in the relevant regulations. The consequence of the interruption is that the limitation period needs to be restarted. Also, the limitation period may be interrupted as a result of the taxpayer's bankruptcy and the application of enforcement

---

11 More about the remission of tax arrears: R. Mastalski, "*Ulgi w spłacie zobowiązań podatkowych,*" [in:] *Ordynacja podatkowa. Komentarz*, eds. B. Adamiak, J. Borkowski, P. Borszowski, R. Mastalski, J. Zubrzycki, Unimex, Wrocław 2017b, p. 427 et seq.; Z. Ofiarski, *Ogólne prawo podatkowe. Zagadnienia materialnoprawne i proceduralne*, LexisNexis, Warsaw 2010, pp. 149–152; J. Małecki, "*Zobowiązania podatkowe w świetle Ordynacji podatkowej,*" [in:] *Podatki i prawo podatkowe*, eds. A. Gomułowicz, J. Małecki, LexisNexis, Warsaw 2010c, pp. 395–401.

measures of which the taxpayer has been notified. Tax obligations secured by a mortgage are not subject to limitation.

2.3.3.3 *Release from Determining and Collecting Tax*

A tax obligation may expire ineffectively as a result of a release from determining and collecting tax in whole or in part. The entity authorised to perform the release is the Minister of Finance who, guided by an important public interest or important taxpayer's interest, determines the type of tax, the period of release and the group of taxpayers concerned by issuing a generally applicable regulation. In practice, by way of regulation, the Minister of Finance can waive the collection of the following: personal income tax on income from the Erasmus+ programme scholarships; corporate income tax on income (revenue) of central banks having no residence or management seated in the Republic of Poland, generated from interest or discount on treasury bonds issued by the State Treasury on the domestic market; personal income tax on benefits received by taxpayers in connection with the participation in free training in palliative or hospice care held by NGOs or professional associations of physicians or nurses and midwives, established and operating in another EU member state.

2.3.3.4 *Exemption from the Duty to Pay a Tax Based on Interpretation*

This type of ineffective expiry of a tax obligation is closely related to the institution of interpretation of the general provision of tax law and the interpretation of the individual provisions of tax law. It should be emphasised that the majority of tax obligations in Poland arise upon the occurrence of a taxable event. As a consequence, there is a need to apply the provisions of tax law correctly in practice. In the meantime, in the Polish volatile and often ambiguous tax reality, the taxpayer's obligation to be familiar with and interpret the provisions of tax law properly is beyond their capacity. The situation is so complicated that, as a result of "under-legislation," two different tax authorities are likely to arrive at different conclusions when facing the same facts and legal background. Due to the fact that the consequences of misapplication of the provisions of law must be accepted by the taxpayer and considering the poor prospects of improvement in the quality of law-making, it was decided to introduce the idea of interpretations into the Polish tax system.

An entity authorised to issue a **general interpretation** is the minister competent in public finances. Their aim is to ensure the uniform application of tax law by the tax authorities. A general interpretation may be issued *ex officio* or on request. When issuing general interpretations, the Minister of Finance should take into account the existing case law of the domestic courts, the Constitutional Tribunal, or the Court of Justice of the European Union. An **individual interpretation** is issued by the Director of the National Tax Information in individual cases at the request of a party concerned (taxpayer, tax remitter, tax collector, or third party). An application for an individual interpretation can refer to the ascertainment of facts or to future events. The party applying for an individual interpretation is obliged to exhaustively present the facts of the case or future events, as well as a personal opinion on the legal estimation of these facts of the case or future events. Having received the application, the Director of the National Tax Information issues an individual interpretation which contains an exhaustive description of the facts or future event and the assessment of the applicant's position along with the legal justification for the assessment. Where the applicant's position is entirely correct, the Director of National Tax Information does not need to include the legal justification. In the assessment of the applicant's position is negative, the individual interpretation of the issuing body states the correct position together with its legal grounds. The applicant may complain against the interpretation to the administrative court. As a rule, individual interpretations are issued without undue delay, i.e. not later than three months from the date of receipt of the application. The provisions of Polish tax law also provide for the so-called "tacit interpretation" where, in the absence of an interpretation within a time limit of three months, it is agreed that, on the day following the cut-off date of issue of the interpretation, such an interpretation is deemed given and fully endorsing the applicant's position.

Obtaining and implementing an individual interpretation, as indicated in the position of the Director of National Tax Information, causes that in the event of amending, expiration or failure to include the interpretation in the process of investigating a fiscal matter, the entity holding the interpretation is released from the obligation to pay the tax related to the event being the subject of interpretation.[12]

It should be emphasised that individual interpretations may also be issued by the mayor, i.e. the first-instance tax authority, on such fiscal matters as: real property tax, forest tax, agricultural tax, tax on the means of transport, or local fees (small trade licence fee, location fee, resort fee, dog fee, advertising fee).

2.4 Liability for Tax Obligations

2.4.1 Introduction

In accordance with the regulations of Polish tax law, there are two categories of entities liable for tax obligations. The first category includes those entities whose liability results from their specific conduct, such as the lowering of the tax base or the failure to perform, for example, to pay tax on time. The entities making up this category are as follows:

– taxpayer;
– tax remitter;
– tax collector.

The other category includes those entities that are held liable not for their own debt but for the tax debt of taxpayer, tax remitter, or tax collector that have failed to pay due tax for various reasons. The entities making up this category are as follows:

– legal successors;
– third parties.

2.4.2 Taxpayer's Liability

The taxpayer is liable for tax obligations up to the value of all its assets. It is therefore a property liability of the taxpayer of unlimited and personal

---

12 More about interpretation: K. Teszner, "*Interpretacje przepisów prawa podatkowego,*" [in:] *Ordynacja podatkowa. Komentarz*, ed. L. Etel, Wolters Kluwer, Warsaw 2017, pp. 169–272; W. Morawski, T. Janicki, "*Urzędowe interpretacje prawa podatkowego,*" [in:] *Nowelizacja Ordynacji podatkowej*, eds. B. Brzeziński, W. Morawski, Wolters Kluwer, Warsaw 2016, pp. 38–57.

nature. This means that the tax creditor is entitled to assert their claims not only on the taxpayer's existing assets available at the time when the tax obligations arises but also on assets that will be acquired by the taxpayer in the future. The taxpayer's liability will continue until the expiry of the tax obligation.

In order to secure the interest of the tax creditor, Polish tax law provides that the liability of a taxpayer who is married covers not only their individual property but also the joint property of the taxpayer and their spouse. Under Polish law, the community of property becomes legally effective upon contracting marriage. Joint property comprises property items acquired during the community period. Besides, joint property includes, among other things, spouses' remuneration for work and income from other gainful activity or income from joint property and individual property of each of the spouses. The individual property of each of the spouses is made up of the following items: acquired by inheritance or gift; used only to meet the personal needs of one of the spouses; copyright and related rights; industrial property rights; obtained by compensation for bodily injury or health impairment; obtained as a reward for the spouse's personal achievements.

2.4.3 Tax Remitter and Tax Collector's Liability

The liability of the **tax remitter** occurs when it fails to fulfil its obligations of calculating, collecting and paying taxes for the taxpayer to the competent tax authority. The provisions of tax law stipulate that the tax remitter is liable for uncollected tax or collected but unpaid tax. Failure to collect tax is the result of the taxpayer's failure to calculate it. On the other hand, failure to pay tax may result from: failure to calculate it, incorrect calculation or calculation and collection followed by non-payment. A tax remitter that has not fulfilled their tax obligations is liable up to all their assets. On the other hand, if the tax remitter is a natural person (e.g. a lawyer employing an office assistant under a contract of employment), they may be liable not only up to their entire assets but also with the joint property of the remitter and their spouse.

It should be noted that, in certain circumstances, the minister competent in public finances may, by issuing a regulation and in cases justified by a valid public interest or valid interests of taxpayers release certain groups of tax remitters from the obligation to collect taxes or tax advances while specifying the deadlines for tax payments to be made independently by the taxpayers.

In addition, the provisions of tax law permit tax remitters to apply to the competent tax authority for release from the obligation to collect tax. This can be the case when the collection of tax may jeopardise the taxpayer's valid interests, in particular their existence. Moreover, the release of the tax remitter from the obligation to collect tax advances may occur when the taxpayer substantiates that the tax to be collected would be disproportionately high in relation to the tax due for the fiscal year or other accounting period.

The specific nature of the institution of **tax collector,** which collects tax from the taxpayer and pays it to the competent tax authority, makes this entity liable up to all their assets for collected but unpaid tax. As in the case of a tax remitter or taxpayer being a married person, the liability of the tax collector may be extended to the property shared with their spouse.

2.4.4 Legal Successors' Liability

There are two categories of legal successors in Polish tax law. The first one includes those successors who have been established as a result of transformation or combination of entities. The other group includes natural persons who are heirs or beneficiaries of a will. The aim of introducing the institution of tax succession into Polish tax law was, on the one hand, to secure the tax creditor's interest by enforcing tax debt from legal successors. On the other hand, tax succession entitles the legal successors to enjoy their predecessors' rights. The lack of tax succession would cause the expiration of such rights as the right to the refund of an overpayment or to appeal against a fiscal decision after, for example, the transformation of a company or death of an individual.

As pointed out above, legal successors may be legal persons established through the combination of: legal persons, partnerships, or partnerships and commercial companies. Legal successors may also be legal persons that are established through the acquisition of another legal person or a commercial company. The newly created entity will be subrogated to all the rights and obligations provided for in the law of each of the combined

persons or companies. Tax succession will also occur after the establishment of a legal person as a result of the transformation of another legal
entity (e.g. transformation of a limited liability company into a joint stock
company) or a company without legal personality (e.g. transformation of
a limited partnership into a limited liability company). Legal succession
also pertains to legal persons performing an acquisition or legal persons
established after a division. Legal successors are also entities acquiring
state-owned enterprises and companies that have acquired or taken over
such enterprises pursuant to the regulations on the commercialisation and
privatization of state-owned companies.

The other category of legal successors includes natural persons who
inherit some assets after the taxpayer. Such persons assume the testator's
property rights and obligations, however, only to the extent stipulated in
the provisions of tax law. It must be emphasised that, with regard to the
non-property rights connected with the economic activity conducted by
the testator, the legislator has conditioned the acquisition of such rights
upon the continuation of the business activity by the heir. The rule is that
tax succession in Polish law applies only to the taxpayer and their successors, yet, by way of exception, it has been extended to the tax remitter for
the acquisition by their successors of non-property rights and obligations
related to the conducted economic activity. As regard the heirs' liability for
the testator's tax obligations, the provisions of the Polish Civil Code apply
pertaining to the acceptance and rejection of inheritance and, by extension,
the liability for debts under the succession. According to Polish law of succession, succession can be accepted or rejected. If the latter is the case, it
is assumed that the heir did not live up to the opening of the succession.
Acceptance of the succession can take place without limiting the liability for
debt, the so-called simple succession, or with a limited liability for debt, the
so-called acceptance under benefit of inventory. A statement of acceptance
or rejection of the succession is made by the heir within six months of the
date of learning about their title to succession. However, it is assumed that
failure to make such a statement within the said time limit is tantamount to
acceptance under benefit of inventory. The way of accepting the succession
will result in the liability for debts under succession. The general rule is that
until the acceptance of the succession, the heir is liable for the debts under

the succession only up to the value of the succession. As from the moment of accepting the succession, they are liable up to the value of their own assets. The unlimited liability for debts under the succession will encumber the heir that will accept the succession directly. On the other hand, in the case of acceptance under benefit of inventory, the heir will only be liable for the inherited debt up to the value of the inventory or the inventory of assets of succession.

From the death of the testator, the period of limitation or refund of an overpayment does not begin and the already begun period is suspended until the date when the decision of the court on the acquisition of inheritance or the registration of the certification of succession becomes effective. However, this cannot take longer than until the second anniversary of the testator's death.

A legal successor is also the beneficiary of a will who has received their due legacy. As a rule, the testamentary legacy in Polish civil law is when the testator, through their testamentary disposition, obliges the statutory or intestate heir to make a specific property performance for the benefit of a named person (beneficiary of a will). The liability of the beneficiary of a will for the testator's tax obligations is limited to the value of the received legacy.[13]

2.4.5 Third Parties' Liability

The concept of liability of third parties for the taxpayer's tax arrears in Polish tax law is specific. It strengthens the position of the tax creditor by making a certain group of entities liable for the taxpayer's debt. The liability of third parties is the aftermath of prior taxpayer's tax obligation. It has, therefore, an accessory and follow-up character. First, the tax authorities offer the opportunity to pay tax by the taxpayers themselves. Only the lack of payment or the risk that the tax obligation might not be fulfilled by the taxpayer properly cause the tax authority to appoint a third party as the person liable for the payment of tax. The appointment of a third party

---

13 M. Zdebel, "*Prawa i obowiązki następców prawnych oraz podmiotów prze-kształconych*," [in:] *Ordynacja podatkowa. Komentarz*, ed. H. Dzwonkowski, C.H. Beck, Warsaw 2016, p. 610 et seq.

as the person liable for the taxpayer's tax debt does not release the latter from the liability to pay their own levies. The position of a third party is specific as they cannot challenge the very legitimacy of the taxpayer's fiscal obligation or the grounds for determination of those items of the tax that have an impact on the amount of the tax burden. Only the taxpayer has the right to do so. Still, a third party may question the grounds for its recognition as an entity liable for the taxpayer's debt and may contest the scope of this liability.

Third parties are liable up to all their assets jointly and severally with the taxpayer for all the taxpayer's arrears. Joint and several liability is the debtors' liability in this case, which means that the payment of tax by either of the entities (taxpayer or the third party) causes the taxpayer's tax obligation to expire. A third party who has paid tax for the taxpayer has the right of recourse.

The tax authority determines the liability of a third party by issuing a tax decision. However, before that, it should enable the taxpayer to pay tax themselves. Therefore, the liability of a third party cannot be enforced, for example, before the expiry of the tax payment deadline, or on the date of service of (i) the decision determining the amount of the tax obligation, (ii) the decision on the refund of an accrued value added tax advance, or (iii) the decision on the taxpayer or tax collector's liability for tax. It should be emphasised that a third party can be made liable not only for the taxpayer's tax arrears but also for the tax remitter and tax collector's arrears. A decision on third party's liability for tax cannot be issued if five years have passed since the end of the calendar year in which the tax arrears occurred. In contrast, in the case of third parties who VAT payers or attorneys of active VAT payers, the decision on the liability of such entities cannot be issued if three years have passed since the end of the calendar year in which the tax arrears occurred.

In addition, the limitation of the liability resulting from the decision becomes effective after three years from the end of the calendar year in which the decision on the third party's liability was served.

The list of third parties is closed, which means that the tax authority may only appoint as third parties those entities that are enumerated in the TOA.[14] A third person can be:

a) **divorced taxpayer's spouse:** such a person is liable jointly and severally with the taxpayer up to all their assets for the taxpayer's arrears related to tax obligations arising over the period of community of property. This means that if there was no community of property between the taxpayer and their spouse during the marriage, the divorced spouse cannot be appointed as the person liable for the taxpayer's tax arrears. It should be emphasised that the Polish legislator has further limited the liability of the divorced spouse up to the value of their share in the joint property.

b) **taxpayer's family member:** such a person is liable up to all their assets jointly and severally with the taxpayer conducting an economic activity for the tax arrears resulting from this activity and arising in the period when the family member cooperated with the taxpayer on a regular basis in the taxpayer's business activities and benefited from that activity. Those persons who, in the period of regular cooperation with the taxpayer, were entitled to the maintenance obligation from the taxpayer – to the extent provided for in the maintenance obligation – are not liable. In Polish tax law, the taxpayer's family members are: descendants, ascendants, siblings, descendants' spouses, stepchildren, and persons in cohabitation with the taxpayer. Clearly, the list of family members omits to include the taxpayer's spouse. This is due to the fact that the taxpayer, as indicated above, is liable for their tax obligations up to their entire assets or joint property if married. But when there is no community of property between the spouses, then the taxpayer's

---

14 See more: R. Mastalski, *Prawo podatkowe*, C. H. Beck, Warsaw 2017a, p. 298 et seq.; A. Olesińska, E. Prejs, "*Odpowiedzialność osób trzecich za zobowiązania podatkowe*," [in:] *Nowelizacja Ordynacji podatkowej*, eds. B. Brzeziński, W. Morawski, Wolters Kluwer, Warsaw 2016, p. 144 et seq.; Z. Ofiarski, *Ogólne prawo podatkowe. Zagadnienia materialnoprawne i proceduralne*, LexisNexis, Warsaw 2010, p. 207 et seq.; B. Brzeziński, *Prawo podatkowe*, Dom organizatora, Toruń 2000a, pp. 125–135.

spouse, if the above conditions are met, will be treated as a person in cohabitation with the taxpayer.

c) **entity acquiring an enterprise or an organised part of an enterprise:** such an entity is liable up to all their assets jointly and severally with the taxpayer for the tax arrears arising up to the date of acquisition of tax arrears related to the conducted economic activity, unless they had been unaware of these arrears while maintaining due diligence. The liability of the acquiring party has been, however, limited to the value of the acquired enterprise or its organised part. In addition, the liability is excluded if the acquisition of the enterprise or its organised part has taken place under the enforcement and bankruptcy proceedings.

d) **single-member capital company:** to regard such a company as a third party it must be established as a result of the transformation of an entrepreneur (natural person) into this company. If this is the case, then such a company is liable up to all its assets jointly and severally with that natural person for the tax arrears related to the conducted economic activity arising until the day of the transformation.

e) **company without legal personality where an individual made a contribution to cover its share:** it is liable up to all its assets jointly and severally with that individual for the tax arrears arising until the in-kind contribution of an enterprise related to the contributed enterprise.

f) **straw party:** a person who has acts as a front for the taxpayer by lending their personal name or company name in order to conceal the taxpayer's actual business or the actual size of the business. Such a person is liable up to all their assets jointly and severally with the taxpayer for any tax arrears arising while conducting this business.

g) **owner, autonomous possessor or perpetual usufructuary of a thing or property right:** such a person is liable for the user's tax arrears arising in connection with their business activity, provided that the thing or right are related to the activity or are conducive to this activity. In this case, the legislator introduced a limitation of the liability of the third party up to the amount equivalent to the value of a thing or property rights in use. The liability of the entities as third parties arises when between them and the users of a thing or property right there are family, capital, or property relationships established or other links under labour relations.

h) **lessee or user of a real property**: such a person is liable up to all their assets jointly and severally with the taxpayer, being the owner, perpetual usufructuary or autonomous possessor, for any tax arrears related to tax obligations arising from the taxation of the property during the term of lease or use.

i) **partner in a civil law partnership and limited liability partnerships from the Code of Commercial Companies and Partnerships**: such a person is liable for the partnership's tax arrears up to all their assets jointly and severally with the partnership and other partners. The appointed third party may also be a former partner but only in relation to those tax arrears whose payment deadline expired when that person was a partner.

j) **members of the management board of capital companies**: they are liable for the tax arrears of the company jointly and severally up to all their assets. Yet, the provisions of tax law assign the liability to the management board members depending on whether the enforcement on the company's assets has proven unsuccessful in full or in part, and whether a member of the management board has not demonstrated that a bankruptcy petition was filed in due time or the reorganisation proceedings were initiated in that time, or failure to file a petition for bankruptcy occurred without that member's fault. In addition, a member of the management board is liable for the company's tax arrears if they fail to point to the company's assets that can be subject to enforcement with a view to repaying the company's debt in its greater part. Yet, the liability of the members of the management board has been limited and covers only the tax arrears for liabilities whose payment deadline expired during their term as members of the management board.

k) **members of the management board of other legal persons**: this group of entities includes, e.g. members of the boards of foundation or associations. They are jointly and severally liable up to all their assets for the tax arrears of legal persons other than capital companies.

l) **company liquidators**: they are liable for the company's tax arrears arising during the liquidation procedure. The liquidators appointed by the court are not liable.

m) **legal persons performing the acquisition or legal persons established as a result of division**: they are jointly and severally liable up to all their assets for the tax arrears of the divided legal person. There is no liability of those legal persons whose property acquired as a result of division or property established as a result of separation comprises an organised part of the enterprise. The liability of the legal persons performing the acquisition or newly-established legal persons is limited to the value of the acquired net assets following from the division arrangement. The liability has also been limited to those arrears that had arisen before the date of separation.

n) **guarantor whose security has been accepted by the tax authority:** such a person is liable up to all their assets jointly and severally with the taxpayer, tax remitter, tax collector, their legal successor or a third party for the obligations resulting from the decision related to the established security, along with delay interest and enforcement costs incurred in the execution of this decision – up to the amount of guarantee or surety and within the time limit specified in the guarantee or surety.

o) **taxpayer in VAT:** such a person is jointly and severally liable up to all their assets for the tax arrears of an entity supplying goods listed in Annex 13 to the Act on Value Added Tax. The annex lists a group of goods that is most often traded in the so-called carousel transactions. The provisions of the Polish Act on Value Added Tax make the liability of the VAT payer dependent on the value of goods purchased from one entity (PLN 50,000) and the fact whether at the time of supply of the goods the taxpayer was aware or had reasonable grounds to believe that the entire or partial amount of tax for the supply of these goods would not be paid to the tax office.

p) **attorney of an active VAT payer:** such a person is liable jointly and severally up to all their assets for tax arrears in value added tax arising from activities performed over six months from the date of registration of the taxpayer as a VAT payer. This liability will occur when the registration of the active VAT payer has been made by the attorney.

3 Tax Proceedings

3.1 Tax Authorities

Polish lax law fails to offer an official (statutory) definition of a tax authority. However, the key legal instrument of Polish tax law, the Tax Ordinance Act (TOA), lists the types of such authorities along with their range of competence. Regardless of the above, there is an option, under other regulations, of granting the powers of tax authorities to other bodies handling various public levies. As of 1 March 2017, a new law has been enacted – the Act on the National Fiscal Administration – which aims to reform the organisation of the existing fiscal structures.[15] The reform mainly addresses the centralisation of the organisational units of individual tax authorities. Instead of the existing bodies organised in three divisions (tax, customs, and tax audit), a new consolidated system of services has been established reporting to the Minister of Finance and referred to as the uniform customs and fiscal administration.

Each tax authority, both within the domain of the central and local administration, exercises its powers under three types of competence:

a) instance competence – it specifies which tax authority is competent to examine and decide a case in the first instance and which tax authority has the power to review this decision in the second instance;
b) material competence – it is understood as the capacity of a tax authority to handle specific types of tax matters, e.g. related to local taxes;
c) local competence – to handle matters in a specific territory of the country.

From 1 March 2017, the new structure of tax authorities within the national fiscal administration is made up of:

---

15 Act of 2 December 2016. Regulations implementing the Act on the National Fiscal Administration (Journal of Laws of 2016, item 1948) and the Act of 16 November 2016 on the National Fiscal Administration (consolidated text: Journal of Laws of 2018, item 508 as amended).

a) the head of the tax office and the head of the customs and fiscal office as first-instance bodies (the former may also act as an appeal body for cases stipulated in the law);

b) director of the fiscal administration chamber as the body accepting appeals against both the decisions of the head of the tax office and the head of the customs and fiscal office.

It should be highlighted that, pursuant to specific regulations, the director of the fiscal administration chamber may also act as a first instance body and then as the appeal body to review their own decisions issued by the same body in the first instance proceedings. Such a solution violates the universal principle of two-instance proceedings.

Moreover, the new fiscal administration has also gained a new tax authority: the Head of the National Fiscal Administration who, as a tax authority, has assumed some of the previous competence of the Minister of Finance, for example, the annulment of decisions, re-opening of proceedings, agreements on the determination of transaction prices, interpretation of tax law (the minister competent in public finance has remained a tax authority in matters related to the interpretation of the general provisions of tax law). The Head of the National Fiscal Administration has also taken over the general supervision over fiscal matters from the Minister of Finance.

The amendments to the law concerning the tax authorities do not apply to local tax authorities. The first-instance tax authorities in local self-governments are: mayor – the head of the municipality, *starosta* – the head of the district, or *marszałek* – the head of the province. The appeal body is the Local Government Board of Appeals.

The scope of powers of the local self-government tax authorities, and therefore also their competence in relation to the subject matter, is set out in separate statutes. In Poland, the *starosta* and *marszałek* use their powers of tax authorities only in relation to fees and other non-tax liabilities. Presently, neither the district nor the province receives income from their own local taxes.

The regulations in question also provide for the option of exclusion of both an employee of or the entire tax authority from deciding a given case. The relevant statute offers detailed justification for these. The exclusion of an employee may take place either *ex lege* or at the request of the employee or the party.[16]

3.2 A Party to Tax Proceedings

A party to tax proceedings is the taxpayer, tax remitter, tax collector or their legal successor as well as other persons who, in order to secure their legal interest, demand the activity of the tax authority to which the activity refers, or whose legal interest the activity of the tax authority relates to.[17] The regulations in question also contain other detailed provisions thereto, for example, covering such cases as spouses who are jointly taxable. In this case, the spouses are one party to the proceedings, and each of them is empowered to act on behalf of the two.

Also, social organization may participate in tax proceedings as a party having received the consent of the person concerned.

A party to tax proceedings may also act through an attorney.

Under the current regulations, the power of attorney may be general, specific or *ad litem*. It may be granted in the form of an electronic document. An attorney may be an individual with full legal capacity to carry out legal transactions. In minor cases arising in the course of tax proceedings, a tax authority may require no power of attorney if the attorney is the party's spouse, and there are no doubts as to the existence and scope of his or her authorisation to act on behalf of the party.

The general power of attorney authorises the individual to act in all tax-related matters and in other matters falling within the competence of the tax authorities. The specific power of attorney authorises the individual to act in a specific tax case or any other specific matter falling within the competence of the tax authority. In Poland, a party to tax proceedings is also required, if they do not appoint a general or specific attorney, to nominate an attorney to receive notices and correspondence if:

---

16 P. Smoleń, "*Organy podatkowe*," [in:] *Ordynacja podatkowa. Komentarz*, ed. H. Dzwonkowski, C.H. Beck, Warsaw 2018, pp. 111–124.

17 M. Masternak, "Nowe pojęcie strony postępowania podatkowego," *Przegląd Podatkowy* 2003, No. 3, p. 48 et seq.; A. Hanusz, "Strony postępowania podatkowego a ciężar dowodu," *Przegląd Podatkowy* 2004, No. 9, pp. 49–54.

a) they change the permanent or habitual place of residence to a place in a non-EU state;
b) they are not domiciled or habitually resident in the Republic of Poland or in another EU member state and submits a request for the initiation of tax proceedings in Poland or has been notified of the initiation of tax proceedings in Poland.

3.3 General Rules Governing Tax Proceedings

The TOA lists a set of general principles of tax proceedings covering the rights and obligations of the tax authorities. Violation of these principles by the tax authorities may result in the commencement of extraordinary procedures and lead, for example, to the re-opening of the proceedings or annulment of the issued decision. The TOA contains the following principles[18]:

1. **The principle of rule of law (legality):** it provides that tax authorities act according to the law. Any action taken by the representatives of the fiscal administration must be rested upon applicable tax law. Tax authorities are required to apply this principle throughout the entire tax proceedings. Observance of the rule of law safeguards the citizens against the lawlessness of tax officials.

2. **The principle of conducting tax proceedings in a manner enhancing confidence in the tax authorities:** it provides that the proceedings should be conducted carefully and correctly. If any doubts arise, they should not be interpreted to the detriment of the taxpayer. If a tax clerk makes a mistake, he or she must not shift the result of the mistake to the taxpayer.

3. **The principle of providing any necessary information and explanation about tax regulations related to the subject matter of tax proceedings:** the tax authorities are obliged to provide a written response to the taxpayer's written inquiry concerning the scope of application of the relevant tax regulations in individual cases which are not subject to any tax proceedings, tax inspection or proceedings before an administrative court.

---

18 Z. Ofiarski, *Ogólne prawo podatkowe. Zagadnienia materialnoprawne i proceduralne*, LexisNexis, Warsaw 2010, pp. 233–248.

4. **The principle of objective truth**: this principle obliges the tax authorities to take all the necessary measures to state the facts and resolve the case. The principle of objective truth is addressed not only to the body deciding the case but also to the appeal body. The tax authorities are required to gather any evidence to prove the facts relevant to the resolution of the case.

5. **The principle of active participation in the proceedings**: this principle provides that the tax authorities should enable the party to the proceedings to take an active part in the proceedings: from the commencement of the proceedings to the final decision of the appeal body (second instance). This entails a special obligation, namely before issuing the decision the tax authorities should allow the party to express their opinion on the collected evidence and material as well as on the requests made.

6. **The principle of explaining the grounds for prerequisites**: this principle obliges the tax authorities to explain to the parties the grounds or justification of the case.

7. **The principle of quick action**: this principle obliges the tax authorities to handle cases thoroughly and quickly. In addition, uncomplicated cases that do not require the collection of evidence should be handled promptly.

8. **The principle of written form**: this principle obliges the tax authorities to resolve cases in a written form. The oral procedure is admissible exceptionally under the special provisions of other laws.

9. **The principle of two-instance proceedings**: this principle entitles each party to appeal to a higher instance through the authority that issued the decision. The principle is derived from the provisions of the Constitution of the Republic of Poland.

10. **The principle of final decision**: this principle protects both the acquired rights and the general legal order, especially with a view to stabilising the latter. The principle of final decision means that decisions which cannot be appealed against are conclusive and effective.

11. **The principle of open proceedings**: this principle guarantees the protection of the parties' privacy and reputation. No other persons than the parties to the proceedings can access and view the records of the case.

3.4 Tax Proceedings: Types and Procedures

In general, tax proceedings are a series of formal steps taken by the tax authorities to examine and resolve a tax case. There are two types of tax proceedings:

a) ordinary proceedings; and
b) extraordinary proceedings which is further divided into three procedures: annulment of the decision, re-opening of proceedings, and revocation or alteration of the final decision. The above proceedings are intended to eliminate final decision from legal transactions. The grounds for the annulment of a decision can be the defective content of the decision. The re-opening of proceedings takes place when some defects are identified in the decision-making proceedings.

All types of proceedings share the same structure: (i) the initiation, (ii) the investigation (collecting evidence), and (iii) the decision settling the case. The decisions taken by the tax authorities can be complained against to the Provincial Administrative Court. On the other hand, the judgement of the court may be referred to the Supreme Administrative Court in Warsaw for cassation.

The initiation of proceedings is either *ex officio* or at the request of the party. The *ex officio* initiation has the form of a resolution. In the case of initiation at the request of the party, the initiation date is the date of submission of the relevant application to the tax authority. The initiation of proceedings at the request of the party is communicated to all the other persons involved in the proceedings as parties. Tax proceedings may also be initiated electronically. If this is the case, the date of initiation is the date of receipt by the tax authority of the relevant request in electronic form. If the proceedings are initiated *ex officio*, the date of initiation is the date of serving the above-mentioned resolution to the party.[19]

The commencement of tax proceedings marks the beginning of all the deadlines related to the case. Also, the tax proceedings principles begin to

---

19 B. Adamiak, "*Wszczęcie postępowania*," [in:] *Ordynacja podatkowa. Komentarz*, eds. B. Adamiak, J. Borkowski, P. Borszowski, R. Mastalski, J. Zubrzycki, Unimex, Wrocław 2017, p. 996 et seq.

apply. Any activities by the tax authorities undertaken before the formal initiation of tax proceedings have no legal effect.

The tax authority may issue a decision refusing the initiation of proceedings. This may happen following a relevant request filed by a person other that the parties or when the proceedings cannot be initiated because of some other reasons. A refusal to initiate proceedings can be complained against.

Any party's applications (requests, clarifications, appeals) should be made in writing, by telegram, teleprinter, fax, electronic means or by means of a form available on the Internet website of the competent tax authority.

The application should meet specific formal requirements in order to be accepted. If it does not, the authority requests the party to remedy the identified deficiencies within seven days. Failure to do so results in the application being rejected. Similarly, if the application does not contain the party's address, it is ignored, and no further request is made to the party.

If the tax authority receiving the application is not competent to examine the case, it should immediately forward the application to the competent one and notify the applicant of doing so. An application submitted to the incompetent tax authority before the deadline set out in the law is regarded as submitted before the deadline.

The investigation (collection of evidence) is intended to establish facts relevant for the provisions of tax law. The ascertainment of facts or lack thereof is part of the evidence-taking procedure. The whole of evidence obtained in this procedure makes up the so-called evidence material. The TOA specifies an open-end set of evidentiary items. According to statute, evidence can be anything that can help clarify the matter and is not illegal. Unless the provisions of law require an official confirmation of certain facts or legal status by a certificate, a tax authority collects a statement from the party, at its request, under the threat of criminal responsibility for false deposition. According to the TOA, evidence in tax proceedings may include, in particular, tax accounts, tax returns submitted by the party, the testimony of witnesses, opinions of experts, etc. The law also adopts the principle of equal effect of evidentiary items, regardless of their nature.[20]

---

20 B. Brzeziński, *Prawo podatkowe*, Dom organizatora, Toruń 2000a, pp. 190–211.

Also, the so-called evidence exclusions were adopted in the law. They provide that the witnesses may not be:

1) persons unable to notice or communicate their observations;
2) persons obliged to keep state or official secrecy, in terms of circumstances that are subject to such secrecy, if they were not exempted from the duty to maintain this secrecy according to the procedure provided for in the provisions in force;
3) priests of legally confirmed religions – on facts that are subject to the seal of confession.

According to the provisions of the law, nobody has the right to refuse to testify as a witness, with the exception of the party's spouse, parents, children, or siblings. The right to refuse to testify also continues after the dissolution of marriage. Furthermore, witnesses have the right to refuse to answer questions if the answers might expose them or their relatives to criminal liability or results in an infringement of a legally protected professional secret.

The tax authority may, in the evidence-taking procedure, use the evidence of the hearing of the party, after receiving their prior consent. If no such consent is given, the hearing is impossible.

Polish law allows the taking of extraordinary evidence. Such evidence comes from the tax information obtained as a result of **the lifting of bank secrecy** at the written request of the tax authority. The tax authorities may exercise this right if, from the evidence collected in the course of tax proceedings, it appears that it is necessary to supplement that evidence or compare it against the information from financial institutions such as banks, insurance institutions, funds, or brokerage houses. The financial institutions listed above are obliged to prepare and share information concerning the party to the proceedings and covering their bank accounts along with their number, the turnover and status of these accounts, concluded credit or loan agreements, shares or bonds purchased through banks from the State Treasury. The request to lift bank secrecy and transfer the requested information by the financial institutions is only possible if the tax authorities have summoned the party to submit the relevant information and the party, within the fixed time limit: (i) did not supply the information; or (ii) did not authorise the tax authorities to request the financial institutions to provide information; or (iii) provided information that requires supplementing or comparing with the information from the financial institutions.

The evidence-taking procedure is governed by **the principle of free assessment of evidence**. The tax authority assesses, based on the entire collected evidence, whether a given circumstance has been proven as fact. Guided by its knowledge, experience, and inner conviction, the tax authority assesses the evidential value of particular evidence items and the effect of proving one circumstance on other circumstances. The free assessment of evidence does not mean that any appraisal is admissible.

The party may request the authority to produce evidence if the evidence is relevant to the case, unless the circumstances are sufficiently confirmed by other evidence. Such a request may be submitted in a number of ways: in writing, by fax, or by e-mail. It should contain a justification or an indication that the production of evidence is central to the resolution of the case. The tax authorities are not obliged to admit any evidence submitted by the party if other evidence items are adequate and sufficient to ascertain facts. The tax authority may set a time limit for the party to submit evidence in their possession. A time limit for the submission is decided by taking into account the nature of the evidence and the status of the proceedings, but it may not be shorter than three days. The party should be informed of the place and date for producing evidence of witness testimony, expert opinions or inspections, at least seven days before the deadline. The party is entitled to participate in producing the evidence, may ask questions to witnesses and experts and can offer explanations.

Before the decision is issued, the tax authority sets a seven-day deadline to express an opinion on the collected evidence. This time limit cannot be shortened or extended, and its ineffective expiry entitles the authority to issue a decision, regardless of the fact that the party has failed to exercise their right.

According to the TOA, the appeal body may conduct a **hearing** as part of the proceedings. This can be done by the tax authority of first instance. A hearing can be either *ex officio* (initiated by the body itself) or at the request of the party.

The tax authority settles the case by issuing a **decision.**[21]

According to the provisions of the TOA, such a decision includes the following:

1) the designation of the tax authority;
2) date of issue;
3) the designation of the party;
4) reference to the legal basis;
5) settlement of the case;
6) the factual and legal justification;
7) instruction of the appeal proceedings – if the decision may be appealed against;
8) signature of the authorised person (along with the full name and official position).

The tax authority issuing the decision is bound by the decision as from the time is has been served to the party.

The party may, within 14 days after being served the decision, request that the decision be complemented.

Besides decisions, in the course of tax proceedings tax authorities issue **rulings**. Rulings address specific matters arising during tax proceedings, but they do not generally settle the case, unless the relevant regulations so provide.

A ruling contains:

1) the designation of the tax authority;
2) date of issue;
3) the designation of the party or other entities involved in the proceedings;
4) reference to the legal basis;
5) settlement of the case;
6) instruction as to whether and under what procedure the ruling can be challenged or complained against before the administrative court;
7) signature of the authorised person (along with the full name and official position).

---

21 W. Chróścielewski, W. Nykiel, "*Postępowanie podatkowe,*" [in:] *Polskie prawo podatkowe,* ed. W. Nykiel, Difin, Warsaw 2013, pp. 123–126.

Basically, a ruling should contain a factual and legal justification. A ruling issued in tax proceedings may be **complained against**. A complaint must be lodged no later than within 7 days of the date of service of the challenged ruling.

A decision of the tax authority issued in the first instance may be **appealed against** to a higher instance. An appeal against the decision of the tax authority should point to the objections against the decision, define the essence and the scope of the request underlying the appeal and should shall indicate the evidence justifying the request. An appeal is lodged with the competent body of appeal via the tax authority which issued the decision. An appeal must be lodged no later than within 14 days of the date of service of the contested decision. If the tax authority issuing the decision finds that the appeal brought by the party deserves to be allowed in full, it will issue a new decision reversing or amending the contested one. The new decision may also be appealed against. The tax authority which received the appeal forwards it, along with the case files, to the appeal body without undue delay (not later than within 14 days as of the receipt of the appeal).

The appeal body issues a decision (i) upholding the decision of the first instance authority, (ii) repealing the decision of the first instance authority, or (iii) discontinuing the appeal proceedings. The appeal body may not decide to the detriment of the appealing party unless the contested decision grossly violates the law or public interest.

3.5 Selected Institutions of Tax Proceedings

3.5.1 Deadlines

According to the TOA, the processing of a case requiring evidence-taking should be held without undue delay, i.e. within no more than a month, and with particularly complex cases no more than two months from the initiation of proceedings. The processing of a case in the appeal procedure should take no longer than two months from the date of receipt of the appeal application by the appeal body. Cases that have been subject to hearing or where the party requested the hearing should be processed no longer than three months. These deadlines are exclusive of (i) the time limits provided for in the provisions of tax law for other specific actions, (ii) periods of suspension of the proceedings and (iii) delays caused by the party or such that are beyond the control of the authority.

In each case of failure to process a case within the prescribed time limit, the tax authority notifies the party of this fact while stating the reason for the failure and proposing a new deadline for handling the matter. The same obligation is also to be fulfilled by the tax authority if the said failure can be attributed to the causes beyond the control of the authority.

The TOA provides for the institution of **reminder**. Recourse to this institution can be had when the authority does not process the case within the statutory time limit or within an additional time limit set by the authority. Reminders are submitted to an authority of a higher instance. The authority of a higher instance which received the reminder will examine the complaint and if it recognises is as justified it sets an additional deadline to the tax authority for settling the case and requires a clarification of the reasons and indication of the persons responsible for not settling the case within the deadline, and, if necessary, undertakes measures preventing any infringement of deadlines for settling the case in the future.

The provisions of the TOA also regulate the liability of an employee of a tax authority who, without justified reason, has not processed the matter by the deadlines or has not performed the obligation under of notifying the party of failure to meet the deadline, or has not settled the matter in the additional deadline. Such an employee is held liable for the breach of order or disciplinary liability or other liability as provided by law. Irrespective of the above, if the time of processing of a case is extended excessively, the party may submit **a complaint on the authority's failure to act** to the provincial administrative court. Such a complaint may be lodged with the administrative court having exhausted the methods of appeal if they have been used by the applicant in the proceedings before the competent authority. The said complaint is not limited by any deadline.[22]

---

22 J. Małecki, "*Postępowanie podatkowe w świetle Ordynacji podatkowej,*" [in:] *Podatki i prawo podatkowe*, eds. A. Gomułowicz, J. Małecki, LexisNexis, Warsaw 2010b, pp. 465–470.

3.5.2 Restoration of a Deadline

In the event of the party's failure to meet a deadline, this deadline may be restored. It can be done upon the application of the interested party if they substantiate that the failure occurred without his or her fault. An application to restore a deadline must be submitted within seven days from the day of the failure to meet it. When submitting the application, the activities for which the deadlines were determined are to be completed.

3.5.3 Service of Notices

The tax authority serves notices against a signed and dated receipt via a postal service, its employees or by persons authorised under separate regulations.[23] If the party so agrees, the service of notices may be held electronically. The party may not suffer the negative consequences of the authority's failure to serve notices appropriately.

Notices are served against a signed and dated receipt. It is a proof of service to the appropriate addressee. The service of notices can be **direct**, i.e. directly to the addressee(s) or **indirect**, i.e. through an adult household member, neighbour, landlord and a person authorised to accept correspondence at the addressee's (party's) workplace. Any refusal to acknowledge the receipt of a notice by the addressee should be recorded by the postal service.

Notices are served on the party or their representative, if applicable. If the party has appointed an attorney, notices are served on the attorney. During the proceedings, the party and its representative or attorney are obliged to notify the tax authority of any change to their mailing address, including the e-mail address. If this obligation remains unfulfilled, a notice is deemed served to the current address, and the tax authority attaches it to the case files.

If the party stays abroad for a minimum two months, it is obliged to nominate an attorney to receive its notices and correspondence. The said obligation also applies to individuals who are not residents in the Republic of Poland.

---

23 M. Kalinowski, M. Masternak, "*Doręczenia w postępowaniu podatkowym*," [in:] *Nowelizacja Ordynacji podatkowej*, eds. B. Brzeziński, W. Morawski, Wolters Kluwer, Warsaw 2016, p. 178 et seq.

Notices are served on individuals in their place of residence or workplace. Notices may also be served at the seat of the tax authority or addressee's workplace on a person authorised by the employer to accept correspondence. If it is not possible to serve notices in any of the ways named above, notices are delivered to the party in any location where he or she may be at the time of service.

In the event of failure to serve a notice directly or indirectly, there is an option of the so-called substitute service. In this approach, the post office or the municipal office retains the notice a period of 14 days. The addressee is notified twice about the awaiting correspondence: every seven days after the first failed attempt to deliver the notice. A notification of correspondence awaiting in the post office or municipal office is placed in the addressee's mailbox or, if not possible, on their house door or on the door of their office or other premises where he or she works, or in another visible location at the entrance to the addressee's property. The correspondence is deemed served after the last day of the 14-day period, and it is attached to the case files.

Legal persons (companies) are served notices in their registered offices or place of business. The receipt of a notice is acknowledged by a person authorised to receive correspondence.

3.5.4 Suspension of Tax Proceedings

The suspension of tax proceedings is based on either obligatory or optional grounds. In accordance with the TOA, the tax authority must suspend the proceedings:

1) in the event of the death of the party, unless the proceedings are discontinued as pointless;
2) if examining the case and issuing the decision depends on considering a preliminary issue by a different authority or court;
3) in the event of death of the statutory representative of the party;
4) in the event of a loss of capacity to legal transactions by the party or a statutory representative;
5) in the case of a third party's liability – until the decision on this liability becomes final and valid;

6) in the case of an application to another country's authorities to transfer information necessary to establish or determine the amount of tax obligation.

Suspension is granted by a ruling which can be complained against.

The optional suspension of tax proceedings takes place when the relevant application is filed by the party, and the proceedings concern the granting of a tax obligation relief.

The tax authority resumes, *ex officio* or at the request of the party, the suspend proceedings when the reasons (obligatory or optional) justifying its suspension have expired. In the event of expiry of the obligatory reasons for suspension, the tax authority resumes the proceedings *ex officio* or at the request of the party. On the other hand, if the optional grounds are no more valid, the proceedings are resumed only at the request of the party.[24]

3.5.5 Penalties

The tax authorities may impose penalties. They may affect the party, the party's attorney, a witness or an expert who, despite the correct summons by the tax authority, has not appeared personally without justified reason or groundlessly refused to provide explanations, issue an opinion, etc. Penalties are in the form of fines paid in cash. They are imposed by a ruling that can be complained against. The deadline for payment of a fine is seven days from the date of service of the ruling.

The tax authority that has imposed the penalty may, at the request of the fined person submitted within seven days from the day of serving a ruling imposing the penalty, may find that the non-appearance or non-performance of other duties to be justified and may reverse the ruling imposing the fine. The imposition or reversal of a fine is decided by the tax authorities in charge of the proceedings.[25]

---

24 M. Bogucka-Felczak, "*Zawieszenie postępowania*," [in:] *Ordynacja podatkowa. Komentarz*, ed. H. Dzwonkowski, C.H. Beck, Warsaw 2016, pp. 1045–1055.
25 S. Presnarowicz, "*Kary porządkowe*," [in:] *Ordynacja podatkowa. Komentarz*, ed. L. Etel, Wolters Kluwer, Warsaw 2017, pp. 1492–1496.

4 Taxes Intended for the State Budget

4.1 Tax on Goods and Services

Value-added tax (VAT) was introduced into the Polish tax system by the Act of 8 January 1993 on Tax on Goods and Services and Excise Tax.[26] Upon Poland's entry in the European Union, a revised law was laid down through the **Act of 11 March 2004 on Tax on Goods and Services**.[27] The statute goes with a broad range of implementing acts defining the operation of this tax in detail. Accession to the European Union runs parallel to the process of the so-called tax harmonization and entails the obligation of a member state to interpret its law in accordance with European Union law. The key EU law addressing this area is **Council Directive 2006/112/EC of 28 November 2006 on the common system of value added tax.**

The **payers** in goods and services tax are entities (legal persons and natural persons) who conduct an economic activity independently, irrespective of the purpose or result of such an activity. The taxable **economic activity** – according to statute – is any activity of producers, traders, or service providers as well as farmers and persons in liberal professions (freelancers). This activity includes, in particular, the use of goods or other values on a continuous basis and for profit-making purposes. In principle, there is no need to register as payer of goods and services tax (submit a declaration). Becoming (or not) such a taxpayer takes place upon the initiation of activities directly attributable to the intended business operations. Registration is required only in the case of agricultural, forestry, or fishing holdings run by more than one person.[28]

To be given the status of a VAT payer, the entity must run a business **independently**. According to the provisions of the Act on Goods and Services Tax, VAT payers are not:

---

26 Act of 8 January 1993 on Tax on Goods and Service and on Excise Tax (Journal of Law No. 11, item 50 as amended).

27 Act of 11 March 2004 on Tax on Goods and Services (consolidated text: Journal of Laws of 2017, item 1221 as amended).

28 J. Matarewicz, *Ustawa o podatku od towarów i usług. Komentarz*, C.H. Beck, Warsaw 2017, p. 197 et seq.

1) persons performing work under labour and similar relations;
2) persons performing work through the so-called personally performed activity (e.g. provision of services under a contract of mandate or contract for specific work);
3) authors and artistic performers remunerated with royalties.

It is worth noting that the statute establishes a specific category of taxpayers: **small taxpayers**. The status of a small taxpayer is given to entities whose gross sales did not exceed the PLN equivalent of EUR 1,200,000 in the previous fiscal year. For taxpayers running a brokerage business managing investment funds, this limit is the PLN equivalent of EUR 45,000. A small taxpayer can choose a tax settlement method based on the approach that the tax liability related to its transactions arises on the day of receipt of the entire or part of the payment (cash basis).[29]

Bearing in mind numerous VAT frauds revealed in the Polish tax system, the Polish legislator is gradually introducing regulations that are intended to minimise state budget losses. One of such regulations broads the list of goods, the supply of which is subject to the reverse charge mechanism (e.g. wire, gold, silver, copper, zinc, electronic integrated circuits, mobile phones, video game consoles or glass, paper, and plastic waste).[30] In addition, the legislator's response to numerous VAT-related offences is the introduction, as of 1 January 2017, of the reverse charge mechanism also in construction services, including works related to the construction of residential and non-residential buildings, construction of roads and motorways, bridges, tunnels, pipelines, power stations, sports stadiums, demolition of works, earthworks, installation of gas piping, plastering, painting, glass and concrete works. The reverse charge mechanism applies to taxpayers providing construction services if the following conditions are met cumulatively: both the service provider and the customer are registered as active VAT payers, and the customer acts in the role of a subcontractor.

---

29 P. Karwat, "*Powszechny podatek obrotowy – VAT,*" [in:] *Prawo podatkowe przedsiębiorców*, ed. H. Litwińczuk, Wolters Kluwer, Warsaw 2017, pp. 639–641.
30 See more: M. Militz, "Odwrotne obciążenie w VAT – wymogi materialne i formalne realizacji prawa do odliczenia podatku naliczonego," *Przegląd Podatkowy* 2018, No. 3, p. 35 et seq.

According to the provisions of the statute, taxable by goods and services tax are:

1) the supply of goods and services for consideration within the territory of the country;
2) exports of goods;
3) imports of goods to the territory of the country;
4) intra-Community acquisition of goods for consideration within the territory of the country;
5) intra-Community supply of goods.

In addition, taxable are goods in the event of dissolution of a civil partnership or company without legal personality or in the event of termination of taxable activities by a taxpayer who is a natural person.

Excluded from taxation are **the transactions of disposal of an enterprise or an organised part of an enterprise** and **activities which cannot be the subject matter of any legally effective agreement** (e.g. drug trafficking or smuggling).

According to the statute, exempt from goods and services tax are, among others, postal services, hospital and medical care, child and youth care, educational and cultural services, or social assistance activities. Some other exempt activities are: the supply of agricultural products by the so-called flat-rate farmer, insurance transactions, financial and real property transactions, the supply of goods related to tax-exempt activities, the supply of postage stamps and duty stamps. The provisions of the law in question also list a considerable number of exemptions related to the **imports of goods.**

The general rule is that the **tax liability** arises upon the delivery of goods or provision of services. However, the statute provides for two derogations. First, the tax liability may occur upon receipt of the entire or partial payment. This is valid for the activities listed in the law, such as: delivery of goods through enforcement proceedings, transfer of the property of goods pursuant to an order of the public authority in exchange for compensation. Second, the tax liability may also arise upon invoicing. This applies to construction or assembly services, delivery of printed books, supply of electricity, heat and refrigeration energy, supply of natural gas as well as services listed in the law, such as telecommunications services, rental, personal security.[31]

The tax base is **everything which constitutes consideration** paid or owed to the supplier of goods or services in connection with the sale from the purchaser, customer or third party, including any surcharges directly affecting the price of the goods or services supplied by the taxpayer. Therefore, the tax base also covers taxes, duties, fees and other charges of a similar nature, as well as commissions, packing costs, transport, and insurance collected by the supplier or service provider from the purchaser or customer. The following are not included in the tax base: rebates, discounts, and reductions and amounts received from the purchaser or customer as a return of substantiated expenses incurred on behalf of and for the benefit of the purchaser or customer and recognised temporarily by the taxpayer in their tax records. The law also provides for the option of lowering the tax base after the transaction has been closed, for example, by the amounts of discounts and reductions or by the value of returned goods and packaging.[32]

In the case of **gratuitous supply of goods**, the taxable amount is the purchase price of the goods or similar goods or, if no purchase price is given, the costs of production determined upon the supply of these goods. Similarly, in the case of **gratuitous provision of services**, the taxable amount is the cost of provision of these services incurred by the taxpayer.

With regard to **the imports of goods**, the taxable amount is the customs value increased by the payable duty. If the imported goods are subject to excise tax, the taxable amount is the customs value increased by the payable duty and excise tax.

The effective **VAT standard rate** in Poland is **22%**. However, it has been raised temporarily (until the end of 2018) to **23%**. This rate is the standard rate. What follows, it applies to all goods and services, except those taxable by other tax rates or VAT-exempt. In addition to the standard rate, some reduced rates have been adopted: **5%** and **7%**. The 7% rate has been increased temporarily to **8%** (until the end of 2018).

---

31 M. Militz, "Nowe zasady powstawania obowiązku podatkowego w VAT – ułatwienia czy utrudnienia?," *Przegląd Podatkowy* 2014, No. 2, pp. 9–17.
32 See more: T. Michalik, *VAT Komentarz*, C.H. Beck, Warsaw 2017, p. 514 et seq.

The characteristic feature of goods and services tax in Poland is the existence of zero **rate**. The zero rate applies to, for example, the exports of goods. This is possible provided that the taxpayer received a certificate of exporting goods outside the territory of the EU before the deadline for submitting a tax return for the given accounting period. The zero rate is also used in the supply of goods and services related to transport, sea fishing, and air transport.

Knowing the tax rate and the tax base allows the calculation of the so-called **output tax**. The taxpayer deducts the **input tax**, i.e. the tax paid in the previous trading period in the prices of acquired goods and services, from the output tax. This is how the amount of tax payable to the tax authority is determined.

For taxpayers who acquire agricultural products and services from flat-rate farmers and receive a lump-sum tax refund, the deductible input tax is that lump-sum refund.

If the amount of input tax is higher than the amount of output tax, the taxpayer is entitled to a refund of the excess amount or to transfer the excess amount to set off against the following accounting period. **The amount of refund** is transferred to the taxpayer's bank account at the bank seated in Poland within **60 days** as of the date of submitting the relevant tax settlement.

According to the statute, taxpayers conducting an economic activity are obliged to calculate and pay tax for **monthly periods**, by the 25th day of the month following the month in which the tax liability arises. Small taxpayers who have selected the so-called cash basis method pay tax for **quarterly periods**, by the 25th of the month following the quarter in which the tax liability arises.

As of 1 July 2018, the so-called **split payment mechanism** has been in place. It is intended to limit fraudulent practices involving VAT and the so-called disappearing taxpayer method. The mechanism is voluntary, yet it is possible that the legislator will make it obligatory in the future. The institution will be available to the buyers of goods or services that have received an invoice with the amount of tax indicated. In this case, invoice payments will be made to two separate bank accounts: the net amount to the supplier's bank account and VAT to the supplier's special VAT account. To encourage taxpayers to use this mechanism, the legislator has offered several preferential solutions. First, taxpayers that opt for the split payment mechanism will be able to get VAT reimbursement within 25 days. Second, no increased interest rate for VAT late payments will apply (see Chapter 2). Third, if the invoice is paid using the mechanism in question, the buyer will not be subject to sanctions provided for in the VAT law and will be immune to the provisions on joint and several liability for taxpayer's tax arrears (see Chapter 2).

Tax can be collected by the tax remitter. This can happen in two cases. First, the tax remitter can be an enforcement authority in enforcement proceedings (e.g. bailiff). Second, in the case of intra-Community acquisition of motor fuels whose production or trading is licensed, the tax remitter can be a registered consignee or a warehouse keeper.

The goods and services tax law provides for special tax payment rules by specific groups of taxpayers. Among them, there are, for example, the taxpayers providing **passenger taxi services**. According to the statute, they can choose a flat-rate taxation scheme, which means **3%** of tax rate (temporarily until the end of 2018: **4%**), without the right to reduce the amount of output tax by input tax.

There is also a special group of taxpayers known as **flat-rate farmers. These are** farmers who supply agricultural products from their own agricultural holding or provide tax-exempt agricultural services. A flat-rate farmer benefits from a tax exemption on the supply of their agricultural products and services as well as being entitled to the **lump-sum tax refund.** The lump-sum tax refund is 7% (until the end of 2018).

4.2 Excise Tax

The currently binding excise law entered into force on 1 March 2009 as the Act on Excise Tax.[33] Like value added tax, excise tax is a price-making solution, as it is included in the price of a product subject to excise duty, which means that it is the consumer who accepts the taxpayer's burden. Yet, excise tax is not levied on services. The provision of services is subject

---

33 Act of 8 December 2008 on Excise Tax (consolidated text: Journal of Laws of 2017, item 43 as amended).

to tax on goods and services. In normative terms, the statute itself has a complex and non-uniform structure.

Taxable persons in excise tax are natural persons and legal persons entering into taxable transactions or engaging in taxable conduct.[34] The special group of taxed entities are:

a) importers of a motor car not previously registered in the territory of the country;

b) intra-Community buyers of such a motor car transferring it to the territory of the country from another Community territory;

c) the first seller in the territory of the country of a motor car not registered in the country;

d) subsequent seller of a motor car not registered in the country if excise tax from the first sale of the same car was not paid in the due amount, and this fact has been confirmed during an inspection or fiscal procedure.

The taxable object was determined by the classification of excise products into five basic groups and referring to Annex 1 to the act containing the list of goods concerned. According to the relevant definition, these are energy products, electricity, alcoholic beverages, tobacco products, and tobacco. Taxable is a relatively broad range of activities, among them: production of excise goods, import of excise goods, intra-Community acquisition of excise goods, the sale of excise goods in the country, the use of certain excise goods for the production of other excise goods or for the needs of the using entity.

The scope of taxable objects in excise tax, such as **motor cars**, covers both foreign trade and activities carried out in the country and related to a motor car. In this case, the subject of excise tax is: import, intra-Community acquisition or sale of such a car in a domestic market transaction. According to the principle of single taxation, excise tax is paid on a vehicle manufactured in the country or imported into the country from a foreign country, i.e. before its first registration. Subsequent domestic sales are subject to taxation if, as part of tax proceedings or a tax inspection, it has been established that the due amount of excise tax has not been paid.[35]

---

34 See more: J. Matarewicz, *Ustawa o podatku akcyzowym. Komentarz*, Wolters Kluwer, Warsaw 2016, pp. 186–197.

35 S. Parulski, *Akcyza. Komentarz*, Wolters Kluwer, Warsaw 2016, p. 142 et seq.

Tax base depends on the type of object of taxation. Tax on excise goods is calculated based on their quantity or value – as in the case of motor cars. The Act on Excise Tax enumerated the tax bases for the individual groups of products as well as clarifying the rules of their determination. For example, in the group of energy products, the unit of tax base may be one litre of a finished energy product or its kilogram; on the other hand, alcoholic beverages are taxed based on hectolitres.[36]

Excise tax follows the proportional scale. The excise tax rates are expressed as **an amount or percentage**. There are also special forms of tax scale. To calculate the excise fee on cigarettes and tobacco, combined amount and percentage rates are used.

Basically, taxpayers calculate the amount of tax independently and submit a monthly return by the 25th day of each month following the taxable month. This applies both to produce taxed with excise duty and motor cars. Sometimes, the taxpayer is obliged to submit a simplified tax return. An exception is that the importers of products subject to excise tax do not submit tax returns but declare how much tax is due in the customs declaration. The tax authorities may determine the amount of excise tax if they manage to prove that the taxpayer has made a mistake in their calculation.

4.3 Gambling Tax

Gaming tax is regulated by an act whose name does not allude to any fiscal solution. This is **the Act on Gambling of 19 November 2009**[37] (also known as Gambling Law). This statute sets forth the terms and conditions of organisation as well as the principles of running a business activity involving the games of chance, betting and slot machines. Somewhat by chance the law regulates the taxation by separate gambling tax. This normative solution stands out among other laws on taxation.

Gaming tax feeds the state budget but its fiscal significance is negligible. It is levied on gambling and poker games held in the form of poker tournaments.

---

36 See more: J. Matarewicz, *Ustawa o podatku akcyzowym. Komentarz*, Wolters Kluwer, Warsaw 2016, p. 645 et seq.; p. 684; pp. 689–690; p. 699; pp 704–717; p. 734 et seq.

37 Act of 19 November 2009 on Gambling (Journal of Laws of 2018, item 165).

There are three categories of **taxpayers** in gambling tax:

a) natural persons and legal persons conducting a gambling activity under a licence or permit;
b) entities organising games falling within the state monopoly;
c) participants of poker games held during poker tournaments.

The taxation in question applies to the legal pursuit of a business activity involving gambling. In the case of a poker tournament, taxation does not refer to the business activity but only to participation in a tournament held in a casino under a granted permit.[38]

The **tax remitter** status is assigned to entities holding the licence for operating a casino in which a poker tournament is hosted. The casino operator pays the players their prizes with gaming tax deducted.

The **taxable objects** in gaming tax are activities falling into two basic categories:

a) the organisation of gambling, excluding promotion lotteries and poker played in a poker tournament;
b) participation in poker games in the form of a poker tournament.

Within the meaning of Gambling Law, **gambling** comprises games of chance, betting and slot machine games. **Games of chance** are games with either cash or non-cash prizes and where the outcome is notably conditional on chance while the terms of the game are set by the game regulations.

Tax base in individual games and bets is established separately and is not aggregated. The tax base distribution is as follows:

1) in a cash lottery, raffle lottery and telebingo – aggregated proceeds from the sale of lottery tickets or other proofs of participation in the game;
2) in number games and betting – the total of states paid;
3) in cash bingo – the nominal value of game numbers purchased by the entity organising the game;
4) poker played in a poker tournament – the amount of the cash prize less by the amount of the tournament entry fee;

---

38 M. Duda-Hyz, "*Podatek od gier,*" [in:] *Prawo podatkowe*, eds. P. Smoleń, W. Wójtowicz, C.H. Beck, Warsaw 2017, pp. 348–350.

5) in slot machine games – the amount of difference between the amount obtained from the exchange of chips or paid at the counter and credited in the machine memory, or paid into the machine and the total of wins achieved by the game participants.[39]

The **tax rates** in gaming tax are expressed in percent, and their level depends on the type of lottery, betting transaction, or game. Some examples of tax rates are as follows:

1) 10% – for raffle lottery and raffle bingo;
2) 15% – for cash lottery;
3) 20% – for number games;
4) 25% – for cash bingo and telebingo, audiotele lottery and poker played in a poker tournament.

Basically, taxpayers calculate and pay taxes **for monthly periods** on their own, the payment deadline being the 10th day of the month following the taxable month. The same time limit applies to the submission of **tax returns**. In the case of taxable participation in a poker tournament, the levy is collected via **the tax remitter**.

4.4 Corporate Income Tax

4.4.1 Taxable Entities

Corporate income tax (hereinafter "CIT") was introduced into the Polish tax system by the Act of 15 February 1992 on Corporate Income Tax.[40] The taxpayers in CIT are **legal persons**, that is, entities enjoying legal personality pursuant to the relevant rules and regulations. Legal persons are capital companies (joint stock companies and limited liability companies), cooperatives, associations, foundations, or state-owned enterprises. Still, the provisions of the statute also exceptionally recognise **entities without legal personality** as CIT payers. This group includes capital companies

---

39 See more: K. Ryszard, *"Podatek od gier,"* [in:] *Gry hazardowe. Komentarz do ustawy o grach hazardowych*, eds. M. Bik, R. Kamionowski, D. Obrępalski, K. Ryszard, C.H. Beck, Warsaw 2013, pp. 210–236.
40 Act on 15 February 1992 on Corporate Income Tax (consolidated text: Journal of Laws of 2017, item 2343 as amended).

in organisation (they enjoy the taxpayer status as from the entry into the companies' register), organisational units without legal personality (e.g. incorporated partnerships with the management centre or seat in the territory of Poland, residential communities, electoral committees, private schools and educational establishments), companies without legal personality with the management centre or seat in other country if regarded as legal persons in their country of registration.[41]

A special type of CIT payer is a **tax capital group**.[42] It should be highlighted that such an entity has a legal and tax personality only under the Act on Legal Person's Income Tax. It may be established by at least two commercial law companies with legal personality. The companies composing the group undertake to enter into an agreement on the establishment of a tax capital group that needs to be notarised. The agreement should be effective for at least three years and should be registered by the head of the tax office. It should be stressed that in order to qualify as taxpayer a tax capital group must cumulatively meet the following conditions:

– all companies making up a group must be seated in Poland;
– the amount of share capital per company cannot be lower than PLN 500,000;
– there must be one controlling company in the group that will be obliged to hold 75% of the share capital of the other subsidiary companies;
– subsidiary companies may not hold shares in the share capital of the other companies in the group;
– companies making up a tax capital group cannot be in arrears with the payment of taxes constituting revenues of the state budget;
– a tax capital group must achieve a share of income in revenue of at least 2% for each fiscal year.

The idea of a tax capital group is that its taxable object subject to income tax is the income earned in the fiscal year that is the surplus of the total

41 B. Kucia-Guściora, "*Podatek dochodowy od osób prawnych*," [in:] *Prawo podatkowe*, eds. P. Smoleń, W. Wójtowicz, C.H. Beck, Warsaw 2017, pp. 400–401.
42 K. Gil, "*Art. 1 a [Podatkowa grupa kapitałowa]*," [in:] *Podatek dochodowy od osób prawnych. Komentarz*, eds. K. Gil, A. Obońska, A. Wacławczyk, A. Walter, C.H. Beck, Warsaw 2017, pp. 14–29.

revenues of all companies making the group over their total losses. Thus, any losses generated by the individual companies in the group are offset by income earned by other companies in the year in which they are incurred and not within five years as in the case of taxation under general terms.

The statute in question differentiates between limited and unlimited tax liability. Unlimited tax liability applies to residents who are taxpayers having their management centre or domiciled in Poland. The consequence of recognition of a given entity as resident is the taxation by income tax of all its income irrespective of the place of its earning. Restricted tax liability applies to non-residents, i.e. entities having no management centre or not domiciled in Poland. Entities subject to restricted tax liability only pay tax on their income earned in the territory of Poland.

Entities exempted from CIT are, but not only: the State Treasury, local self-government units, the National Bank of Poland, budgetary units, the National Health Fund, state special purpose funds, state executive agencies, international enterprises and other economic subjects established by the state administration body under international agreements; the Banking Guarantee Fund, the National Insurance Institution, National Fund for Environmental Protection and Water Management.

4.4.2 Taxable Object

The taxable object of CIT is **income**, regardless of the type of source. Income is the surplus – achieved in the fiscal year – of the total revenue over the costs of raising that revenue. Where the costs of raising revenue exceed the total revenue, this difference is known as **loss**. If so happens, the taxpayer is entitled to deduct the amount of loss from the income earned over the nearest, consecutive five fiscal years. However, the deduction in any of these years may not be more than 50% of the amount of such loss.

The correct determination of income or loss, the tax base and, consequently, the amount of due tax requires taxpayers to keep accounts in accordance with the provisions of the Accounting Act.

Exceptionally, the concept of CIT provides for **revenue** as an object of taxation. This exception applies to the revenues generated by non-residents. These revenues include: interest, copyright or related rights, rights to invention designs, trademarks and decorative patterns, payments for providing services consisting of shows, entertainment or sports activities performed by legal persons having their seats abroad, organised through natural persons or legal persons carrying on the activity based on artistic, entertaining and sports events within the territory of the Republic of Poland; performances in the field of advising, accounting, market research, legal services, advertising, management and control, data processing, employees recruitment and personnel obtaining services, guarantees and suretyships, and performances of similar nature, due payments for the transportation abroad of loads and passengers accepted for carriage in Polish harbours by foreign sea trading enterprises, except for transit loads and passengers. In addition, taxable is also the revenues from participation in the profit of legal persons.

As of 1 January 2015, the concept of income tax was supplemented by solutions intended to prevent the transfer from Poland by resident taxpayers of their income to countries with less rigid taxation system. The mechanism provides that taxable is the income of a foreign controlled company in the part corresponding to the shares held conferring the right to participate in the profits of that company after deducting the amount of the dividend obtained by the taxpayer from the foreign controlled company or the amount of disposal by the taxpayer for consideration of their share in the foreign controlled company.

Exclude from CIT are the revenues: from agricultural activity, silviculture, of marine entrepreneurs and related to activities which may not be the subject matter of a legally effective contract.

The basic concepts indispensable for the proper establishment of income are the revenue and allowable expenses (also known as revenue earning costs or tax deductible expenses). The Act on Corporate Income Tax fails to provide the legal definition of revenue. In accordance with the general rule, it is assumed that **revenue** is received cash, pecuniary value and other benefits or performances enumerated in the statute, such as: the value of received things or rights; the value of returned receivables, previously set aside as uncollectible or remitted and included in allowable expenses; revenues earned in connection with the repayment or receipt of a loan (credit facility); taxpayer's remuneration received as a result of redemption of shares (stock) acquired in exchange for a contribution in kind, i.e. contribution of an enterprise or an organised part of an enterprise; the equivalent value of dissolved or reduced provisions, previously recognised as allowable expenses.

Bear in mind that revenue does not always come with the receipt of cash, pecuniary value or other benefits of performance enumerated in the statute. In the case of business activity and special sectors of agricultural production, revenues will also be receivables not actually received, excluding the value of returned goods, compensations and discounts. In such a case, the date of revenue will be the date of issue of a thing, the sale of a property right or the performance of a service, or partial performance of a service, no later than the date of invoicing or the date of payment.

According to the provisions of the Act on Corporate Income Tax, **allowable expenses** are expenses incurred to earn business income or preserve or secure a source of revenue. Therefore, in order for a given expense to qualify as allowable, a causal link must be proven between the expense and its purpose.[43] The law indicates that the purpose may be only to earn income and secure or preserve a source of revenue.[44] It should be emphasised that some types of expenses were denied in the law as allowable even if some causal link can be shown between them and the income earned. These include, among others, the expenses incurred on or due to: the acquisition of land or perpetual usufruct of land; payment of income tax, tax on extraction of certain minerals, special hydrocarbon tax; enforcement procedures related to non-performance; receivables written off as uncollectible; delay interest for late payment of budget receivables; redemption of bonds less the amount of discount; redemption of receivables, except for those previously posted as due revenues; employer's spending on social programmes; losses resulting from the loss or liquidation of vehicles and their post-accident repairs if the vehicles are not covered by a voluntary insurance; maintenance of in-company social facilities, in the part covered by the company social benefit fund; unpaid contributions to the National Insurance Institution; tax on some financial institutions; contributions to the bank guarantee fund.

It should be pointed out that on 1 January 2017 new rules were introduced on the recognition of expenditure as allowable expenses. According

---

43 W. Pietrasiewicz, M. Romańczuk, *Koszty uzyskania przychodów*, C.H. Beck, Warsaw 2009, pp. 2–33.

44 H. Litwińczuk, "*Ustalanie dochodu przedsiębiorców. Zasady ogólne,*" [in:] *Prawo podatkowe przedsiębiorców*, ed. H. Litwińczuk, Wolters Kluwer, Warsaw 2017, p. 114 et seq.

to the new approach, taxpayers conducting a business activity do not include in their allowable expenses that portion of the expense that exceeds the equivalent of PLN 15,000 if the expense-generating payment was not made to a bank account.

Where the taxpayer acquires assets in the form of tangible fixed assets[45] and intangible fixed assets,[46] whose initial value exceeds PLN 10,000, they perform depreciation or amortisation of such assets.[47] Under the applicable laws, the taxpayer can conduct depreciation/amortisation based on:

– **straight-line method**: applicable when depreciation/amortisation write-offs are made consistently throughout the depreciation period. This is the elementary depreciation/amortisation method.[48] This method includes **an accelerated straight-line approach**: applicable when tangible fixed assets are used in specific conditions or environments (e.g. heavy-duty or demanding conditions causing faster wear and tear). It involves the application of factors raising the annual depreciation rates. There is also an option of **individual straight-line method**: applicable to tangible fixed assets purchased as second-hand or upgraded. In such a case, the statute

---

45 Tangible fixed assets are structures, buildings and premises as separate ownership, machinery, equipment and means of transport and other items which: (i) are owned or co-owned by the taxpayer; (ii) have been generated internally; (iii) are complete and in working order on the day of acceptance for use; (iv) their expected useful life is more than one year; (v) are used by the taxpayer for the purposes of their business or are put into use under a lease, tenancy, or rental agreement.

46 Intangible fixed assets are, among others, cooperative member's ownership right to residential premises, cooperative right to utility premises, copyright or related property rights, licences that have been acquired; are fit for economic use on the day of acquisition; have an expected useful life of more than one year; are used by the taxpayer for the purposes of their business or are put into use under a sublicence, lease, tenancy, or rental agreement.

47 More about amortization/depreciation: H. Litwińczuk, "*Ustalanie dochodu przedsiębiorców. Zasady ogólne,*" [in:] *Prawo podatkowe przedsiębiorców*, ed. H. Litwińczuk, Wolters Kluwer, Warsaw 2017, p. 178 et seq.

48 In relation to amortization of intangible assets, the legislator provided that the period of write-downs may not be shorter than: for software licences, copyright, and licences to display films and broadcast radio and television programmes – 24 months; for costs incurred for completed development works – 12 months; for other intangible assets – 60 months.

provides for the minimum depreciation periods whose duration depends on the value of an asset.

- **declining balance depreciation method**: applicable to tangible fixed assets such as special-purpose machinery and equipment and all means of transport excluding passenger cars. This method permits increased depreciation write-offs over the first years of use as a result of increased depreciation rates by a factor not higher than two. Where the value of the allowed tax instalment becomes lower than the instalment determined in the straight-line method, the taxpayer is obliged to make depreciation write-offs by means of the straight-line method.
- **one-off depreciation method**: applicable to taxpayers beginning their economic activity or the so-called small taxpayers.[49] One-off depreciation/ amortisation can only be made in the fiscal year in which the assets were entered in the records of fixed assets, but the total amount of accrued depreciation write-offs cannot, on a one-off basis, exceed the equivalent of EUR 50,000 in that fiscal year. In August 2017, a mechanism was put in place that allows the stimulation of investments made by entrepreneurs. It entails a one-off depreciation/amortisation also by those taxpayers who are neither small taxpayers nor start a business activity. Every year and on a one-off basis, they can settle expenditure on fixed assets of up to PLN 100,000 where the minimum value of such expenditure is PLN 10,000. Exempt are also the revenues earned from the sale of the entire or part of real property making up an agricultural holding. In this case, to obtain preferential treatment, the land sold must not lose its agricultural character.

Besides exemptions related to taxable persons, the concept of CIT also allows for **exemptions related to the object of taxation**. Thus, tax-exempt are, for example, income from the sale of all or part of real property belonging to an agricultural holding; income of ecclesiastical legal persons earned from non-economic statutory activities or from other activities, in the part intended for: religious worship, education, science, culture, care

---

49 Entities that did not exceed the value of receipts from sales (including the amount of due tax goods and services) in the previous fiscal year equivalent to the PLN value of EUR 1,200,000.

and charity and preservation of monuments; taxpayers' income from economic activity, including from the special sectors of agricultural production, in the part intended for an agricultural activity; income of sports clubs allocated to and expended in the fiscal year or the following year for the training of the youth; income of public benefit organisations, in the part intended for statutory activities; income from licensed raffle lotteries and raffle bingo; interest on income or funds collected on fixed-term bank deposits; income from business activities carried out in a special economic zone under the licence; direct payments under the Common Agricultural Policy of the European Union; income of trade unions and social and professional farmer organisations, farm chambers, chambers of commerce, craftsmanship self-government organisations, cooperative audit associations, employers' organisations, and political parties.

4.4.3 Tax Base and Tax Deductions

The tax base in CIT is income or, sometimes as indicated elsewhere, revenue. The concept of CIT provides for the option of **lowering the tax base** by tax deductions provided for in the law. Consequently, the taxpayer may deduct from the tax base the following[50]:

a) **donations** to support religious worship and public benefit organisations. The above preference cannot exceed 10% of income earned by the taxpayer. Moreover, it should be noted that under separate laws regulating the State–Church relationships there is a possibility to deduct unlimited donations, provided that they are donated to the charity and care activities conducted by churches and religious organisations legally operating in Poland;

b) in the case of banks: 20% of the **amount of credit (loans)** redeemed in connection with the implementation of the restructuring programme, classified as uncollectible credit (loan) and recognised as an allowable expense;

c) **eligible costs** incurred by the taxpayer for research and development. The deductible amount cannot exceed the total income earned on

---

50 P. Małecki, M. Mazurkiewicz, *CIT. Podatki i rachunkowość*, C.H. Beck, Warsaw 2017, pp. 1090–1104.

business operations in the fiscal year. Eligible costs include, among others: remuneration and national insurance contributions paid for the personnel conducting research and development activities; acquisition of materials and raw materials directly related to the R&D activities; expert opinions, consultancy services, acquisition of scientific research; paid use of research equipment; costs of obtaining and maintaining a patent. In the case of taxpayers holding the status of R&D centres, the amount of possible deduction may not exceed 150% of the eligible costs enumerated in the statute and incurred by such centres. In contrast, other taxpayers must observe the threshold of 100% of such costs. The deduction is made in the tax return for the fiscal year in which the eligible costs were incurred. If it is not possible to make a deduction in the given fiscal year (due to loss or if the amount of income is lower than permitted deductions), then deductions are made in tax returns for six consecutive fiscal years. As of 1 January 2017, taxpayers who, in the year of starting their business, incurred a loss or earned income less than the permitted deductible amount and, consequently, are unable to deduct the amount of the relief are qualified to a direct refund of eligible costs incurred calculated as the product of the not deducted relief and the tax rate applicable to that taxpayer in the given fiscal year.[51]

4.4.4 Tax Scale and Tax Rates

The tax rates in CIT fall under the proportional tax scale. The basic tax rate is **19%**.

It is worth noting that as of 1 January 2017 small taxpayers and taxpayer beginning their economic activity are qualified, over the first year of their operation, to the tax rate of **15%**. However, the preferential tax rates are not available to, for example, tax capital groups or taxpayers who have been established as a result of transformation of an entrepreneur who is a natural person and conducts an economic activity personally or a partnership or company without legal personality.

---

51 W. Dmoch, *Podatek dochodowy od osób prawnych. Komentarz*, C.H. Beck, Warsaw 2017, pp. 616–621.

Non-residents are liable to lump-sum corporate withholding tax at the rate of **20%** in relation to revenues earned on due charges for the exports of goods and transport of passages by foreign sea navigation companies or revenues earned in Poland by foreign air navigation companies. For other revenues earned by non-residents, the **10%** rate applies. Dividends and shares in the profit of legal persons seated in the Polish territory are taxed at the rate of **19%**.

4.4.5 Minimum Income Tax on the Value of Commercial Facilities

As of 1 January 2018, the so-called minimum income tax on the value of commercial facilities was incorporated into the CIT structure. The new regulation addresses a commonly held belief that economic operators avoid tax payable for the activity of office rental and large-area trade. Hence, the regulation requiring an entrepreneur to pay a minimum amount of income tax if they use high-value assets. It should be emphasised, however, that the taxpayer will only face the tax burden if they do not earn adequate income subject to income tax.[52]

The taxable object is the revenue from the ownership of a fixed asset located in Poland whose initial value exceeds PLN 10,000,000. However, the legislator constrained the taxable object by pointing to only two categories of fixed assets:

– commercial and service facilities classified in the Classification of Fixed Assets (CFA) as: shopping centres; department stores, independent stores and boutiques; other commercial and service premises;
– office buildings classified in the CFA as office buildings.

The tax base is the revenue corresponding to the initial value of the fixed asset on the first day of each month, based on the records kept, less the amount of PLN 10,000,000. The amount of tax for each month is 0.035% of the tax base. Taxpayers are obliged to pay the tax to the competent tax authority by the 20th day of the month following the month for which the tax is paid. However, the amount of tax calculated for a given month is

---

52 More about the new regulations: P. Banasik, A. Kałążny, W. Morawski, "Minimalny podatek dochodowy od wartości obiektów komercyjnych – wybrane problemy," *Przegląd Podatkowy* 2018, No. 2, p. 33 et. seq.

deducted by taxpayers from a CIT tax advance (see Section 4.4.6). However, if it appears that the amount of tax is lower than the tax advance for a given month, taxpayers may not pay the tax. In addition, the law provides that the amount of the tax paid and not deducted in the fiscal year is deducted from CIT calculated for the fiscal year.

The tax is not levied on fixed assets with no depreciation write-offs carried out as well as those that exclusively or mainly satisfy the taxpayer's own needs.

It should be emphasised that, as a result of preliminary consultation with the European Commission, the Polish Ministry of Finance is planning to modify the minimum taxation on commercial property. First, only those structures and buildings will be subject to tax are put in paid use under, e.g., rental, tenancy, or lease agreement. Second, the PLN 10 million threshold rule will be modified and will apply to a taxpayer regardless of the number of structures or buildings in their possession, unlike it is today when it applies to every building. Third, all structures and buildings will be subject to tax. Only residential premises developed as part of governmental and self-governmental programmes addressing social housing will be excluded. Four, a tax payer will be able to apply to the tax authority for the return of minimum tax paid over the amount of due corporate income tax or personal income tax.

4.4.6 Payment Terms and Procedure

The final tax settlement is held after the end of the fiscal year (generally a calendar year). Still, the law provides that a taxpayer may decide that their fiscal year will be a different period of 12 successive calendar months. With this end in view, the taxpayer must amend their statutes, deed or articles of association or other document regulating their operation. Certainly, the taxpayer must advise the head of the tax office of the adoption of a different fiscal year scheme.

During the fiscal year, taxpayers are required to pay advances on annual tax. The rule is that tax advances are paid by the 20th day of each month for the previous month. However, small taxpayers and start-up businesses may, over the first year of their operation, pay tax advances quarterly by the 20th day of the month following the taxable quarter.

The law also provides for a simplified form of payment of tax advances as 1/12 of the output tax shown in the tax return for the preceding fiscal year. Before opting for this simplified scheme, the taxpayer must notify the competent tax authority of their choice at the time of payment of the first tax advance.

Small taxpayers starting a business activity are eligible for the so-called **tax credit**. Tax credit involves a release from the obligation to pay tax advances in the fiscal year following the first fiscal year of activity (if it has lasted for at least 10 full calendar months) or after the second fiscal year of activity if the business was operating for a shorter period in its first year. Taxpayer's release from the obligation to settle tax advances does not release the taxpayer from the obligation to submit an annual tax return. However, the tax shown in the annual tax return is paid over the following five fiscal years immediately following the year in which the release was granted, at the rate of 20% of the output tax shown in the return. To take advantage of tax credit, the taxpayer must submit with the competent head of the tax office a written statement regarding the credit by the 20th day of the month of the fiscal year covered by the release.

Besides paying their monthly CIT advances, taxpayers are also required to make an annual settlement of the tax in their tax return. It should be submitted by the end of the 3rd month of the year following the fiscal year. For non-resident taxpayers, the tax is collected by tax remitters responsible for making payments.

4.5 Personal Income Tax

4.5.1 Taxable Persons

Personal income tax ("PIT") was introduced into the Polish legal system by the Act of 26 July 1991 on Personal Income Tax.[53] **The taxpayers** are **natural persons**. If they are domiciled in Poland, they are subject to unlimited tax liability. This means that taxation covers the total income (revenues), irrespective of the location of the source of income. Natural persons not domiciled in Poland are subject to limited tax liability, i.e. the tax is levied

---

53 Act of 26 July 1991 on Personal Income Tax (consolidated text: Journal of Laws of 2018, item 200, as amended).

only on their income (revenues) earned in the Polish territory. According to the provisions of tax law, a person domiciled in Poland is one who has their centre of personal or economic interest (the so-called "centre of vital interests") in Poland or has been staying in the Polish territory for more than 183 days in the fiscal year.[54]

The taxpayers are also **partners** in partnerships (except in incorporated partnerships). Revenues generated by a partnership, as well as its expenses, are attributed to each partner commensurately to their right to participate in partnership's profit.

Natural persons' income tax is a personal tax; therefore, the rule is that each person is liable to separate taxation of his or her income. However, in certain circumstances, the legislator has allowed exceptions to this rule.[55]

The first exception is related to spouses. In the vast majority of cases, married persons are economically regarded as one. Therefore, the concept of PIT allows for **joint taxation of married couples.** In order to qualify for this solution, the married couple must remain married for the entire fiscal year and must have a community of property. Joint taxation of married couples permits that the due tax is assigned to both spouses in double the amount of the tax calculated from half of their total income after they have separately deducted all the reliefs from their respective income. Taking advantage of this solution is also possible when once of the spouses earns no income or their income is below the tax-free amount. The joint taxation scheme is also available to spouses who are not Polish residents but are domiciled in one of the states of the European Union, the European Economic Area, or the Swiss Confederation. This preference will also be available to spouses, one of whom is a Polish resident and the other is domiciled in one of the states mentioned above. In both cases, a prerequisite to take advantage of the joint taxation preference is the certificate of residence and earning taxable revenue in Poland of at least 75% of the total revenue generated by both spouses during the fiscal year.

54 B. Kucia-Guściora, "*Tax Residence in the Polish Personal Income Tax System – Major Problem Areas*," [in:] *Selected Issues in Taxation and Tax Authorities in Central Europe*, ed. P. Smoleń, Wydawnictwo KUL, Lublin 2016, pp. 17–29.
55 R. Mastalski, *Prawo podatkowe*, C.H. Beck, Warsaw 2017a, pp. 409–413.

The second exception applies to **a single parent or legal guardian** raising minor children, children with disabilities or school-age children up to 25 years of age. In such a case, the tax burden is established as double the amount of tax calculated from half of the single parent's income. This scheme can be used by single parents residing in another member state of the European Union, any state of the European Economic Area or in the Swiss Confederation, having the certificate of residence and having earned taxable revenue in Poland of at least 75% of their total revenue generated in the given fiscal year.

It should be noted that in accordance with the applicable law the income of own and adopted minors, except for the income of their work, scholarships and income from items transferred to them for free use, is added to the parent's income. In Poland minors are persons below 18 years of age.[56]

4.5.2 Taxable Object

Taxable by PIT are all kinds of income raised by a taxpayer in the fiscal year overlapping with the calendar year. In Polish tax law, **income** is the surplus – achieved in the fiscal year – of the total revenue from a given source over the expenses incurred to raise that revenue. However, with regard to specific types of activity and events (e.g. special sectors of agricultural production, business activity), the Act on Natural Persons' Income Tax provides for specific methods of determining income.

In accordance with the provisions of the Act on Personal Income Tax, revenue is the money and pecuniary values received or put at the taxpayer's disposal in a calendar year, and the value of benefits in kind and other non-gratuitous benefits. The revenue received by the taxpayer is recognised on the accruals or cash accounting basis. The former cover revenues from the economic activity, special sectors of agricultural production, some money capitals and disposal of things or rights for consideration. Other sources of revenue are recognized on the cash basis.

In order to determine income, the key element, besides the amount of revenue, is the correct determination of allowable expenses. The Act on

---

56 A. Goettel, *Podatkowoprawne skutki zawarcia i ustania małżeństwa*, Wolters Kluwer, Warsaw 2016, pp. 239–242.

Natural Persons' Income Tax stipulates the so-called **actual costs**. In such a case, the taxpayer deducts the actual expenses if incurred in order to generate revenue or to preserve or secure the source of revenue. In addition, the concept of Polish PIT also includes **lump-sum deductions**, expressed in amount or percentage (e.g. revenues from employment relationships).

Where allowable expenses are higher than the total revenue, the resulting difference is a **loss** from the source of revenue. The rule is that a loss can be deducted from income in the subsequent fiscal years. But to make this happen, three conditions must be met. First, income may be reduced only by a loss generated in the same source. Second, a loss may be diminished over immediate five successive fiscal years. Third, the size of deduction in any of these years may not be more than 50% of the amount of loss.

For social reasons or to avoid the risk of double taxation, the legislator excluded certain revenues from taxation. These include: revenues from activities that cannot be the subject matter of any legally effective contract (e.g. prostitution, fencing, drug trafficking); revenues from the division of the joint property of spouses; revenues from agricultural activity; revenues from silviculture, or revenues subject to the provisions governing inheritance and gift tax.

The rule is that the taxpayer's income earned during the fiscal year and originating in different sources are aggregated. Then, taxable is the **total income from all sources of revenue**. Nevertheless, some income generated in the sources of revenue indicated in the statute are not aggregated. In such a case, the taxpayer is obliged to submit a separate tax return showing the income earned and the amount of output tax. The concept of PIT offers as many as ten sources of revenue.[57] It happens that the rules of determining income, allowable expenses or tax rates are established separately for each of these sources.

---

57 R. Mastalski, *Prawo podatkowe*, C.H. Beck, Warsaw 2016, pp. 422–430.

4.5.2.1 Employment Relationships and their Equivalents

Revenues from employment relationships and their equivalents, such as service relationship,[58] outwork relationship,[59] and the cooperative employment relationship[60] are all cash payments and pecuniary value of benefits in kind or their equivalents, regardless of the source of funding of these payments and benefits, in particular: basic salary, overtime remuneration, various allowances, awards, cash allowances for unused holiday and any other amounts, regardless of whether fixed in advance, and also the cash benefits incurred for the employee as well as the value of other unpaid benefits or partially paid benefits.[61]

This source of revenue also covers pension benefits, i.e. the amount of pension, including the amount of old-age funded pensions, along with any increases and bonuses, excluding family and nursing supplements and additional payments to a family allowance pension for a double orphan.

Tax-exempted are, among others: interest for late payment of salary; the cost of service outfit (uniform) or cash equivalent for this outfit; cash equivalents for tools, materials or equipment use by employees in the performance of their work and owned by them; benefits received by employees for the shuttle service organised by the employer; allowances and other benefits related to the employee's business trip; benefits from the company social benefits fund related with the employee's children attendance to crèches, day-rooms, or kindergartens; the value of benefits granted by the employer for the employee's professional training and development; benefits received by pensioners in connection with their previous employment relationship, service relationship or cooperative employment relationship; death allowance and funeral allowances; aid payments received in the case

---

58 The so-called service labour relation pertains to all uniformed services, i.e. police officers, Border Guard, Prison Service, or professional soldiers.

59 Under an outwork contract, one party undertakes to perform work and deliver the outcomes of this work to the other party.

60 The cooperative work relation is linked to the membership in a cooperative. This kind of work relation can only be established with a cooperative member.

61 J. Marciniuk, *Podatek dochodowy od osób fizycznych. Komentarz*, C.H. Beck, Warsaw 2017, pp. 144–174; R. Styczyński, *Wynagrodzenia pracownicze i inne przychody*, Difin, Warsaw 2015, p. 24 et seq.

of one-off fortuitous events, natural disasters, long-term illness or death within the limit provided for by statute.

If an employee receives certain benefits in kind, their pecuniary value is determined according to the average sales prices of such benefits applicable to other customers. On the other hand, in the case a non-cash benefit that the employee is entitled to for the use of their company car for private purposes, a lump-sum amount is adopted as provided for in the law, its level being contingent upon the car engine capacity.

Income from a service relation, labour relation, outwork relation and the cooperative work relation is established as follows: **allowable expenses**, expressed as a lump-sum deduction, are deducted from the taxpayer's revenue. Such a monthly deduction amounts to PLN 111.25. On the other hand, if the taxpayer's workplace is located outside their place of domicile, this amount is PLN 139.06. The amounts given above are increased if the taxpayer simultaneously generates revenues from more than one service relation, labour relation, cooperative work relation, or outwork relation. If the annual allowable expenses costs are lower than the cost of expenditure on commuting to work by public transport, the taxpayer may recognise these costs in their annual tax settlement at the level actually incurred if proven by the named season tickets.

4.5.2.2 Personally Performed Activity

Personally performed activity is not defined in the Natural Persons' Income Tax Act. The legislator only enumerated specific activities that are deemed to be performed personally.[62] This is debatable as part of the listed activities may be pursued both under an employment relationship (e.g. journalist, sports coach) and as a business activity (e.g. a translator serving as a court expert). Still, the legislator's intention when proposing this source of income was to isolate revenues from work performed on one's own account. The revenues from activities performed personally are very diverse. **Group one** includes revenues from personally perform artistic, literary, scientific, coaching, education or journalist activity, including from participation in

---

62 A. Mariuk, A. Taudul, "Przychody z działalności wykonywanej osobiście," *Przegląd Podatkowy* 2004, No. 7, pp. 22–25; J. Marciniuk, *Podatek dochodowy od osób fizycznych*, C.H. Beck, Warsaw 2017, pp. 175–193.

science, art and culture, or journalism competitions as well as revenues from sports, athletic scholarships awarded under the law and the revenues of referees in sports competitions. **Group two** comprises revenues from the activities of the clergy earned from other sources than the contract of employment (e.g. religion teacher at school). **Group three** includes revenues from the activities of Polish arbitrators partaking in arbitration procedures with foreign partners. **Group four** covers revenues generated by persons performing social or civic work, irrespective of the method of their appointment, including compensation obtained for lost earnings. **Group five** comprises revenues of persons who have been commissioned by a central or local authority body, central or local administration, court or public prosecutor, under applicable law, to perform specific action, in particular the revenues of experts in court proceedings, investigation and administrative proceedings, as well as the tax remitters and tax collectors of public debts; and revenues from participation in committees appointed by a central or local authority body. **Group six** includes revenues earned by persons, irrespective of the method of their appointment, who are members in management boards, supervisory boards, committees or other executive bodies of legal persons and revenues earned by the members of the National Media Council. **Group seven** includes revenues from the performance of services under a civil-law contract of mandate[63] or contract for specific work.[64] **The last group** includes revenues earned under company management contracts, managerial or similar contracts.

The following are **exempt** from taxation: the value of official and sports attire of a member of the Olympic and Paralympic national team; allowances and cost reimbursements received by persons performing social and civic duties up to the amount indicated in the law; cash benefits from the state budget paid to the members of the Polish sports team participating in the Olympic Games.

The **income** from the personally performed activity is determined by deducting the revenue earning costs from the amount of revenue. **Actual**

---

63 A civil law contract under which one party (accepting mandate) undertakes to perform a specific legal transaction for the other party (principal).
64 A civil law contract under which the performing party accepts the performance of a specific work and the contracting party undertakes to pay for it.

allowable expenses apply only to the determination of income from the activities of the clergy. In order to determine the income from other personally performed activities, the **lump-sum deductions** apply. For example, the monthly allowable expenses of PLN 111.25 are applicable to (i) managerial contracts, (ii) company management contracts, (iii) revenues earned by the members of management boards, supervisory boards, committees or other executive bodies of legal persons, and (iv) revenues of Polish arbitrators participating in arbitration procedures with foreign partners. In all other cases, allowable expenses are set at 20% of earned revenue.

4.5.2.3 Economic Activity

Under the Act on Natural Persons' Income Tax, economic activity is defined as a profit-gaining activity in the field of production, construction, commerce, services; prospecting, exploration and extraction of minerals, and the use of things and intangible fixed assets. This activity must be conducted on one's own behalf, regardless of its results, in an organised and uninterrupted manner. In addition, the revenues earned from it cannot be included in other sources of revenue. It should be noted that for a given activity to be classified as an economic activity it cannot meet the so-called "negative conditions" laid down by the legislator. In other words, a natural person may not be recognised as an economic operator if all the following conditions are met:

– liability towards third parties for the result of economic activities and for their performance is borne by the party commissioning the performance;
– economic activities are performed under the supervision and in the place and time specified by the commissioning party;
– the person performing the activities does not assume the economic risk connected with the economic activity.

Revenues generated from an economic activity are amounts owed, even if not actually received, excluding the value of returned goods and awarded discounts.[65] Where the taxpayer sells goods and services liable to VAT, the

---

65 K. Radzikowski, "Pojęcie przychodu należnego z działalności gospodarczej w ustawach podatkowych," *Przegląd Prawa Publicznego* 2009, No. 11, pp. 81–92.

revenue of this sale is the amount less due VAT. It should be noted that the revenue is "amount owed," that is, the amount occurring in the situation when the performance (e.g. payment) becomes due. Thus, in the case of economic activity revenues the moment of performance is not as crucial as the moment of its maturity (accrual method). As the date of revenue, the Act on Natural Persons' Income tax considers the day of handover of a thing, the disposal of a property right or performance of a service, or partial performance of a service, no later, however, than the date of invoicing or the date of effecting the payment. In the case of so-called continuous services settled in taxable periods, the date of revenue is the last day of the taxable period specified in contract or on invoice not less frequently than once a year. On the other hand, if the taxpayer earns revenue that does not fit into any of the methods shown above, the day of receipt of cash payment is considered the date of revenue.[66]

In principle, economic activity revenues are amount owed from the sale of goods or services. Other revenues in economic activity income are, for example: revenues from the disposal of tangible fixed assets or intangible fixed assets for consideration; subsidies, grants, supplements; exchange differences; received contractual penalties; interest on cash held on settlement accounts; the value of returned receivables set aside as uncollectible; the value of received benefits in kind and other free benefits; remuneration of tax remitters for the timely payment of taxes to the state budget; revenue from lease, sublease, tenancy or subtenancy agreements for assets related to the economic activity and other similar agreements; cash received by a partner of the partnership without legal personality for withdrawal from that partnership; received compensation for damage to assets related to the economic activity.

Taxpayers conducting an economic activity are obliged to keep accounting records, i.e. **a revenue and expense book** as a simplified form of accounts-keeping or an account book when the net revenues from the sale of goods and products and from financial operations for the previous fiscal year exceed the PLN equivalent of EUR 2,000,000.

---

66 M. Chudzik, "Zasady powstawania przychodów z działalności gospodarczej," *Monitor Podatkowy* 2006, No. 12, pp. 22–26.

If the taxpayers keep a revenue and expense book, their **income** from the economic activity is the difference between the revenue and allowable expenses plus or minus the difference between the value of the initial and final stocktaking. On the other hand, in taxpayers who keep a ledger, the income from their business activity is the income shown in the properly kept accounts.

Allowable expenses are expenses incurred to earn business income or preserve or secure a source of revenue. Therefore, in order for a given expense to qualify as allowable, a causal link must be proven between the expense and its purpose.[67] The law indicates that the purpose may be only to earn income and secure or preserve a source of revenue. It should be emphasised that some types of expenses were denied as allowable even if some causal link can be shown between them and earned income.[68] These include, among others, expenses on the acquisition of the right to perpetual usufruct; the payment of income tax, inheritance and gift tax, tax on extraction of selected minerals, special hydrocarbon tax; enforcement costs related to non-performance; fines and financial penalties imposed in criminal proceedings, fiscal and criminal proceedings; administrative proceedings; contractual penalties; representation expenses, in particular for catering services and the purchase of food and beverages, including alcoholic beverages; the value of the taxpayer, their spouse and minors' own work.

Where the taxpayer acquires assets (tangible fixed assets and intangible fixed assets) whose initial value exceeds PLN 10,000, they perform depreciation or amortisation write-offs. Under the applicable laws, the taxpayer can conduct depreciation/amortisation based on:

- **straight-line method**: applicable when depreciation/amortisation write-offs are made consistently throughout the depreciation period.[69] This is

---

67 A. Gomułowicz, *Prawna formuła kosztu podatkowego*, Wolters Kluwer, Warsaw 2016, pp. 34–49; M. Pogoński, *Koszty uzyskania przychodów w podatkach dochodowych (PIT, CIT)*, C.H. Beck, Warsaw 2014, pp. 23–38.

68 B. Brzeziński, "Z problematyki ograniczenia możliwości uznania wydatku za koszt uzyskania przychodu," *Kwartalnik Prawa Podatkowego* 2000b, No. 1, pp. 101–107.

69 In relation to amortization of intangible assets, the legislator provided that the period of write-downs may not be shorter than: for software licences, copyright, and licences to display films and broadcast radio and television

the elementary depreciation method. This method includes **an accelerated straight-line approach**: applicable when tangible fixed assets are used in specific conditions or environments (e.g. heavy-duty or demanding conditions causing faster wear and tear). It involves the application of factors raising the annual depreciation rates. There is also an option of **individual straight-line method**: applicable to tangible fixed assets purchased as second-hand or upgraded. In such a case, the statute provides for the minimum depreciation periods whose duration depends on the value of an asset.

– **declining balance depreciation method**: applicable to tangible fixed assets such as special-purpose machinery and equipment and all means of transport excluding passenger cars. This method permits increased depreciation allowances over the first years of use as a result of increased depreciation rates by a factor not higher than two. Where the value of the allowed tax instalment becomes lower than the instalment determined in the straight-line method, the taxpayer is obliged to make depreciation write-offs by means of the straight-line method.

– **one-off depreciation method**: applicable to taxpayers beginning their economic activity or the so-called small taxpayers.[70] One-off depreciation can only be made in the fiscal year in which the assets were entered in the records of fixed assets, but the total amount of accrued depreciation write-offs cannot, on a one-off basis, exceed the equivalent of EUR 50,000 in that fiscal year. In August 2017, a mechanism was put in place that allows the stimulation of investments made by entrepreneurs. It entails a one-off depreciation also by those taxpayers who are neither small taxpayers nor start a business activity. Every year and on a one-off basis, they can settle expenditure on fixed assets of up to PLN 100,000 where the minimum value of such expenditure is PLN 10,000. Exempt are also the revenues earned from the sale of the entire or part of real property making up an agricultural holding.

---

programmes – 24 months; for costs incurred for completed development works – 12 months; for other intangible assets – 60 months.

70 Entities that did not exceed the value of receipts from sales (including the amount of due tax goods and services) in the previous fiscal year equivalent to the PLN value of EUR 1,200,000.

In this case, to obtain preferential treatment, the land sold must not lose its agricultural character.

4.5.2.4 Special Sectors of Agricultural Production

Special sectors of agricultural production are a specialised agricultural activity in which, unlike in the traditional agricultural activity (excluded from taxation), the land factor acts as a place of production rather than a means of production.[71] What follows, in order for income to be qualified as originating in a special sector of agricultural production, it should first be acknowledged that that taxpayer operates within the confines of agricultural activity. They must therefore produce plant or animal products in the unprocessed (natural) state out of their own crops, breeding or rearing, and also must conduct an activity involving the keeping of the purchased animals and plants over normatively defined minimum periods during which their biological growth occurs. However, in order for their revenue to be qualified as falling within a special sector of agricultural production, the activity must be specialised, that is, must correspond to one of the following: cultivation in greenhouses and heated plastic cloches, cultivation of mushrooms and mushroom spawn, *in vitro* cultivation of plants, breeding and rearing of poultry for hatching and poultry meat, poultry hatcheries, breeding and rearing of fur and laboratory animals, breeding of earthworms, breeding of entomophagous insects, breeding of silkworms, apiary keeping and breeding of other animals outside the agricultural holding.

The provisions of Polish law stipulate two methods of establishing **income** from special sectors of agricultural production. **First**, it can be established on a lump-sum basis by multiplying the estimate standard of the annual income assigned to each crop or breeding recognised as a special sector of agricultural production by the number of animals kept or the area of crops during the fiscal year. This is how the annual taxable income is assessed. **Second**, the income from special sectors of agricultural production can be established on the accounting records maintained by the taxpayer,

---

71 See more: M. Burzec, "*Taxation of Specialist Agricultural Activity in Poland – an Attempt to Evaluate the Existing Solutions,*" [in:] *Essential Problems with Taxation of Agriculture*, eds. M. Burzec, P. Smoleń, Wydawnictwo KUL, Lublin 2017c, pp. 51–63.

e.g. a revenue and expense book or the accounts, as provided in the Accounting Act. Where the taxpayer elects to keep the accounts, the income (loss) from the special sectors of agricultural production is determined as the difference between the revenue from these sectors and the allowable expenses incurred, plus the value of the increase in livestock at the end of the fiscal year as compared with the beginning of the same year and less the value of livestock losses during the fiscal year. The choice of the taxation method is the taxpayer's. However, if the net proceeds from the sale of goods, products and from financial operations for the previous fiscal year were at least the PLN equivalent of EUR 2,000,000, the taxpayer is obliged to keep an account book.

4.5.2.5 Rental or Lease Agreements

This category includes revenues earned from rental or lease agreements, property rights and similar arrangements. The primary revenue on rental or lease is the rent. The revenue may also include such expenses incurred by the tenant that go beyond the minor expenses associated with the normal use of the rented or leased property.[72]

Income from rental or lease is the revenue less allowable expenses, i.e. costs (expenses, fees, etc.) incurred for the object of rental or lease.

4.5.2.6 Capital Gains

Capital gains are: interest on loans; interest on deposits, cash in bank accounts and other types of savings; interest (discount) on securities; dividends and other revenues from participation in profits of legal persons; revenues from participation in capital funds; revenues from the sale of shares (stock) and securities and from the exercise of securities rights; revenues from the sale of pre-emptive rights; proceeds of members of occupational pension schemes; the value of contribution laid down in the company statutes, deed or articles of association or another document of a similar nature if a contribution in kind is made to a company/partnership or cooperative;

---

72 T. Kosieradzki, "*Najem*," [in:] *Opodatkowanie nieruchomości*, eds. T. Kosieradzki, R. Piekarz, B. Janiak, Wolters Kluwer, Warsaw 2016, p. 98 et seq.

revenues from the sale of derivative financial instruments and the exercise of the rights thereto.

Tax-exempt are, among others: interest on securities issued by the State Treasury and bonds issued by the local self-government units; interest or discount on bonds issued by the State Treasury and offered on foreign markets and income from the disposal of those bonds for consideration obtained by natural persons; revenues from a contribution in kind if contributed is an enterprise or an organised part of an enterprise; revenues from contributions paid to a company/partnership and returned by the partners in the amount specified in PLN on the date of contribution.

In most capital gains earned by the taxpayer, there are no allowable expenses, and **the tax** on the generated revenue (income) is collected by the tax remitter (e.g. bank) as a **lump sum**.

On the other hand, in the case of disposal of securities and shares for consideration, **income** is established by reducing the revenue by expenses incurred on the takeover or acquisition of such securities or shares.[73]

Capital gains (income) are not aggregated with other income. **The tax rate** in revenues (income) from financial capital is **19%**.

4.5.2.7 Property Rights

The Act on Personal Income Tax has an open-ended catalogue of revenues from property rights. The statute mentions, in particular, the revenues from copyright and related rights, rights to invention designs, rights to the topography of semiconductor products, trademarks and decorative designs, including the disposal of these rights for consideration. An open-ended list of revenues means that a revenue from property rights will be any revenue with its direct source in a property right.

Income from property rights is established by reducing the revenue by its earning costs. In the event of an author generating proceeds from the transfer of a right or licence fee for the transfer of the application of the right to, e.g.: ownership of an invention, topography of a semiconductor products, utility design, industrial design, trademark or decorative design,

---

73 M. Pogoński, "Zakres kosztów uzyskania przychodów w związku z odpłatnym zbyciem papierów wartościowych," *Monitor Podatkowy* 2015, No. 7, pp. 16–20.

allowable expenses are a lump sum of 50% of the earned revenue. On the other hand, if the case of revenues from the use by authors of copyright and by performing artists of related rights or their disposal of such rights, the revenue earning costs amount to 50% of the earned revenue, but they are calculated on the revenue reduced by the national insurance contributions collected by the tax remitted in a given month (pension and accident security contributions).

It should be stressed, however, that the 50% lump-sum deduction in a given fiscal year cannot exceed of the amount corresponding to the upper limit of the first bracket of the tax scale (PLN 85,528).

4.5.2.8 *Disposal of Real Property and Other Items*

In the case of **disposal of real property or its parts for consideration** and share in real property, cooperative member's ownership right to residential or office premises or the right to a single-family dwelling in a housing cooperative, or the right of perpetual usufruct of land, tax liability (i.e. revenue) arises only if the paid disposal is made before the expiry of the period of five years from the end of the calendar year in which the acquisition or construction of the property occurred.

In the case of **other items** (e.g. car), revenue arises when there is a disposal of such items for consideration before the expiry of a 6-month period, counting from the end of the month in which the acquisition occurred.

It should be noted that in the case of disposal of property and other items for consideration, **revenue** is established in a somewhat different manner. The revenue is the actual amount of cash received by the taxpayer, but it is the value expressed in the price given in the agreement less the costs of sale (e.g. the cost of advertising in the press, the commission paid to the real property agency).

Income from the paid disposal of real property is determined by deducting the actual incurred costs from the revenue. The type of deductible expenses depends on the manner of acquisition of property. If a real property has been acquired free of charge, then **allowable expenses** are any substantiated expenses that have increased its value, incurred at the time of ownership and the amount of inheritance and gift tax paid. On the other hand, when a property has been acquired for consideration, **allowable expenses**

are substantiated costs of acquisition or substantiated costs of manufacturing, plus any documented expenses that have increased the value of the real property and property rights, incurred at the time of ownership.[74]

Taxpayers who dispose of a real property for consideration are qualified for **exemption**. In order to take advantage of it, the revenue from the paid disposal of a real property and property rights must be spent on the so-called housing purposes (e.g. purchase of an apartment, house, building plot, repayment of a mortgage) in Poland, in any EU country, in the European Economic Area or in Switzerland. Such spending should be made no later than within two years after the end of the fiscal year in which the disposal took place.

Exempt are also the revenues earned from the sale of the entire or part of real property making up an agricultural holding. In this case, to obtain preferential treatment, the land sold must not lose its agricultural character.

The income earned from the paid disposal of a real property is not aggregated with other incomes, and the applicable tax rate is **19%**.

On the other hand, **income from the disposal of other items for consideration** (e.g. car) is the difference between the revenue earned from the sale and the cost of acquisition of an item, less the value of expenses incurred during the ownership of the item. Income earned in this way is aggregated with other incomes.

4.5.2.9 Income from the Activity of a Foreign Controlled Company

This category of incomes covers **income from the activity of a foreign controlled company** for a period prescribed in the law, in such a part that corresponds to the shares held conferring the right to participate in the profits of that company after deducting the amount of the dividend obtained by the taxpayer from a foreign controlled company or the amount of disposal by the taxpayer for consideration of their share in a foreign controlled company.

Income from the activity of a foreign controlled company is not aggregated with other incomes. The applicable tax rate is **19%**.

---

74 More: K. Kleiber, "Koszty uzyskania przychodów z tytułu zbycia nieruchomości," *Nieruchomości* 2015, No. 4, pp. 31–38.

4.5.2.10 Other Sources

Revenues from other sources are those revenues that cannot be attributed to any of the sources named above. Hence, the statute offers an open-ended list of revenues. The list contains, in particular: amounts paid after the death of a member of an open pension fund; amounts returned from an individual retirement security account and payments from an individual retirement security account; cash benefits from national insurance; maintenance; scholarships, grants, awards and other gratuitous benefits that cannot be assigned revenues from named sources. Besides, revenues from other sources are those proceeds that are not reflected the disclosed sources or originating in undisclosed sources,[75] as well as due, even if not actually paid, revenues from agricultural production related to wine production by farmers producing less than 100 hectolitres of wine during the fiscal year. As of 1 January 2016, revenues from other sources have also been the revenues above PLN 20,000 earned by farmers from the sale of plant and animal products from the farmer's own crops or breeding, processed differently than by means of industrial processing.

Tax-exempt are, among others, scholarships received from the state budget; scholarships for learners and students received from local self-government units or public benefit organisations up to the amount specified in the law; subsidies, grants, supplements and other non-financial benefits or partly financial benefits received for an agricultural activity from the state budget, local self-government budgets or from government agencies; wins and prizes awarded to learners for the participation in competitions, tournaments and contests organised under the Act on the Education System; maintenance allowance for children under the age of 25 and children with disabilities of any age; maintenance allowance for persons other than children granted pursuant to a court's judgement or settlement, up to the amount of PLN 700 per month.

---

75 More: K. Kandut, *Opodatkowanie dochodów nieujawnionych jako narzędzie uszczelniające system podatkowy*, Wolters Kluwer, Warsaw 2017; D. Strzelec, *Opodatkowanie przychodów nieznajdujących pokrycia w nieujawnionych źródłach przychodu lub pochodzących ze źródeł nieujawnionych*, C.H. Beck, Warsaw 2015.

Income from other sources is revenue less allowable expenses. In the case of sale of processed plant and animal products from the farmer's own crops or breeding and from agricultural production of wine by farmers, allowable expenses are established on the basis of the actual expenditure incurred by the taxpayer. On the other hand, in the case of revenues earned under a contract governed by the provisions of civil law (contract of mandate or contract for specific work), the allowable costs are set at 20% of the revenue earned.

It should be stressed that for some revenues raised by taxpayers (e.g. scholarships, maintenance allowance, prizes, wins) allowable expenses do not apply.

4.5.3 Tax Base and the Amount of Tax

The tax base is the total of income earned during the fiscal year. According to statute, the taxpayer is qualified for **deduction** of the following amounts from the tax base:

a) national insurance **contributions** (pension, sickness insurance, accident security insurance);

b) **payments** to the individual retirement security account made by the taxpayer in the fiscal year;

c) **refunds** made in the fiscal year for unduly collected tax that previously increased the taxable income, in the amounts covering the collected income tax if such refunds were not deducted by the tax remitter;

d) expenses incurred by the taxpayer for the use of **the Internet,** up to the amount of PLN 760 in the fiscal year. This deduction is available to the taxpayer only for two successive fiscal years unless they have used it in the preceding period;

e) **donations** made to religious worship, blood donations and public benefit purposes; deduction can be made in the amount of the actual donation, however no more than the amount equal to 6% of the taxpayer's income;

f) **rehabilitation** expenses and expenses intended to facilitate basic functions, incurred in the fiscal year by a taxpayer who is a person with disabilities or a taxpayer maintaining persons with disabilities. These expenses include, among others: conversion and fit-out of residential premises and buildings as required by the disability, payment for a rehabilitation holiday; purchase of medicine; fees paid to a sign language interpreter; paid and necessary transport to obligatory treatment and rehabilitation; maintenance of a service dog by the blind and the visually impaired and persons with a motor disability belonging to the 1st invalidity (upper limit PLN 2,280.00);

g) **eligible expenses**, i.e. allowable expenses spent on R&D activities carried out by the taxpayer. The deductible amount cannot exceed the total income earned on business operations in the fiscal year. Eligible costs include, among others: remuneration and national insurance contributions paid for the personnel conducting the R&D activities; acquisition of materials and raw materials directly related to the R&D activities; expert opinions, consultancy services, acquisition of scientific research; paid use of research equipment; costs of obtaining and maintaining a patent. In the case of taxpayers holding the status of R&D centres, the amount of possible deduction may not exceed 150% of the eligible costs enumerated in the statute and incurred by such centres. In contrast, other taxpayers must observe the threshold of 100% of such costs. The deduction is made in the tax return for the fiscal year in which the eligible costs were incurred. If it is not possible to make a deduction in a given fiscal year (due to loss or if the amount of income is lower than permitted deductions), then deductions are made in tax returns for six consecutive fiscal years. As of 1 January 2017, taxpayers who, in the year of starting their business, incurred a loss or earned income less than the permitted deductible amount and, consequently, are unable to deduct the amount of the relief are qualified for a direct refund of eligible costs incurred in the amount of 18% of undeducted allowable expense (if the taxpayer performs tax assessments according to a tax scale) or 19% of undeducted allowable expense (if the taxpayer is bound by the 19% tax rate).

After making the deductions specified above, the **tax assessment base** is obtained. Income tax is levied on the tax assessment base according to the following **scale**:

Tax assessment base in PLN		Tax is	
Over	To		
	85,528	18%	minus tax reducing amount
85,528		PLN 15,395.04 + 32% of excess amount over PLN 85,528	

Tax-reducing amount is an indirectly stated tax-free amount. Beginning with 1 January 2017, the value of this amount depends on the level of tax assessment base. This scheme is shown below:

a) PLN 1,400 – for tax assessment base below PLN 8,000;
b) PLN 1,400 reduced by the amount calculated according to the formula: PLN 883.98 × (tax assessment base - PLN 8,000) ÷ PLN 5,000, for the tax assessment base above PLN 8,000 and below PLN 13,000;
c) PLN 556.02 – for tax assessment base above PLN 13,000 and below PLN 85,528;
d) PLN 556.02 reduced by the amount calculated according to the formula: PLN 556.02 × (tax assessment base - PLN 85,528) ÷ PLN 41,472, for tax assessment base above PLN 85,528 and below PLN 127,000.

If the personal income tax has been calculated in line with the applicable scale, then the taxpayer is qualified for the following tax deductions:

a) the amount of **health insurance contribution** incurred in the fiscal year directly by the taxpayer or collected by the tax remitter (e.g. employer). The amount of the health insurance contribution that reduced the output tax cannot exceed 7.75% of the contribution assessment base;
b) the amount of **child relief** for every minor **child** (i) that remained under parental responsibility of the taxpayer during the fiscal year; (ii) for whom the taxpayer acted as legal guardian if the child lived with them; (iii) or for whom the taxpayer acted as a foster family. Besides, the allowance is available to a child with disability, regardless of his or her age, and a learning child until 25 years of age. The amount of relief depends on the number of months during which the taxpayer exercised their parental authority, guardianship or care during the fiscal year and on the number of children. For one minor child, the deductible amount

is PLN 92.67 per month, provided that the income of the married taxpayer and their spouse did not exceed the amount of PLN 112,000 in the whole fiscal year. If the taxpayer is a single person, this limit is PLN 56,000. If the limits given above are exceeded, the deducible amount for one child does not apply. For two minor children, the amount of relief is PLN 92.67 per child; for three and more minor children, the amount is: PLN 92.67 PLN for the first and second child, PLN 166.67 for the third child and PLN 225 for the fourth and each further child. Taxpayers earning an income (over the whole fiscal year) that is too low to allow the deduction of the entire amount of child allowance are qualified for the refund of the unused part of the allowance. However, the amount of the refund cannot exceed the total of national insurance and health insurance contributions deducted by the taxpayer in their annual tax return.

This method of tax assessment does not apply to incomes that **are not aggregated** (e.g. income from the sale of property, income from financial capital). Such income, as pointed out earlier, is taxed at the rate of **19%**. In this case, the taxpayer is not qualified for tax-reducing reliefs or allowances.

The **19%** tax rate applies to the taxable income of a taxpayer **conducting an economic activity** or involved in **special sectors of agricultural production** if they choose such a taxation method and report it to the competent tax authority by 20 January of the fiscal year. The choice of this taxation method means that the taxpayer is denied the joint taxation of married couples scheme and loses the option of deductions from income as well as from tax, save for the deduction of social insurance contributions, payments to the individual retirement security account and health insurance contributions.

The concept of this tax also provides for a **"sanction"** rate. It amounts to **75%** and is levied on **revenues** not reflected in the disclosed sources or earned from undisclosed sources.[76]

---

76 K. Kandut, "*Opodatkowanie dochodów nieujawnionych oraz potrzeba i kierunki ich zmian,*" [in:] *Potrzeba i kierunki reformy podatków dochodowych w Polsce,* ed. A. Pomorska, Wydawnictwo KUL, Lublin 2016, pp. 75–108.

It should also be stressed that income tax may be assessed as a **lump sum** on income (revenue). This method is adopted, among others, in the case of tax on income (income) earned by non-residents (e.g. **20%** rate levied on revenues from a personally performed activity or **10%** rate levied on revenues earned by foreign air navigation companies); income from financial capital (**19%** rate levied on, for example, interest on loans) or lump sums levied on the revenues of residents (e.g. **75%** rate levied on savings gathered on more than one individual retirement security account).

4.5.4 Payment Terms and Procedure

Personal income tax is established based on a tax return and payable until **30 April** of the year following the fiscal year. In addition, up to the **20th day of each month** following the taxable month, the taxpayer is required to pay a tax advance to the competent head of the tax office. The advances may be paid by the taxpayers or through the tax remitter. The obligation to pay advances by the taxpayer alone is imposed on those taxpayers who earn income from economic activity, special sectors of agricultural production; rental or lease. Still, the law releases taxpayers who are "first-time" economic operators from the monthly obligation to pay PIT advances once they meet the formal requirements of the relevant regulations. This relief is afforded in the fiscal year immediately following the year in which the taxpayer established their business (if the activity was carried out by at least 10 full months) or for two years immediately following the year in which the activity began (if, over the first year, the activity was carried out by less than 10 full months). The collection of tax advances by the tax remitter, chiefly companies or pension institutions, takes place when the taxpayer earns income from an employment relationship or pensions and in most cases when earning income from personally performed activities.

4.6 Simplified Forms of Personal Income Tax

4.6.1 Lump Tax as a Simplified Form of Taxation

The 1991 Natural Persons' Income Tax Act marked the beginning of the evolution of the Polish taxation system. As opposed to its predecessor, the concept of tax in the new law was rested on the principle of universality.

Although it replaced as many as five taxes related to income earned by the taxpayer, this does not follow that it fully suffices as a solution in terms of the taxation of income (revenue). No doubt, this tax is a key component of the tax system, but it is applicable in parallel with corporate income tax or the so-called simplified forms of taxation of natural persons' income. These include:

a) fixed-rate tax (the so-called taxpayer's card);
b) lump tax on inventoried revenues;
c) lump income tax on the revenues of the clergy.

A standard lump tax does not require the determination of the size of taxpayer's income (revenue) and its value is a fixed amount independent of the actual income (revenue). Basically, the simplified forms of taxation should only complementary to the standard general taxation rules. An example of a typical lump-sum tax is the fixed-rate tax. Paying taxes at a fixed rate is a right and not obligation of the taxpayer and is vested upon the taxpayer's request. The income (revenue) so taxed is not summed up with the income or revenue from other sources that are subject to personal income tax. The proceeds from the fixed-rate tax feed the municipal budgets. Discussed below are the following: lump tax on inventoried revenues and lump income tax from the revenues of the clergy. The regulations applicable to fixed-rate tax will be discussed in the section on levies intended for the municipal budgets.

4.6.2 Lump Tax on Inventoried Revenues

The concept of lump-sum taxation on inventoried revenues is laid down in the Act on Lump-Sum Income Tax on Certain Revenues Earned by Natural Persons.[77]

Lump-sum taxation on inventoried revenues is available to **taxpayers** earning revenue from the sources listed in the statute. These are as follows:

---

77 Act of 20 November 1998 on Lump-Sum Income Tax on Certain Revenues Earned by Natural Persons (Journal of Laws of 2017, item 2157 as amended).

1) natural persons earning revenue from lease, rental or other agreements of similar nature, unless these agreements are concluded as part of a non-agricultural economic operation;
2) natural persons earning revenue from a non-agricultural economic operation;
3) natural persons earning revenue from the sale of self-grown or self-bred plant and animal products processed in a way other than industrial processing, breeding or rearing, with the exception of plant and animal products obtained from the activity in special sectors of agricultural production and products subject to excise tax. Yet, this group of taxpayers are exempt from taxation of their revenue earned in the fiscal year up to the limit specified in the law.[78]

Natural persons who intend to take advantage of this form of taxation in a given fiscal year submit to the head of the tax office having jurisdiction over the taxpayer's place of residence a relevant statement by 20 January of the fiscal year. Where a taxpayer begins their non-agricultural economic activity, such a statement should be submitted no later than on the date of earning first revenue. If the non-agricultural business has a form or a company or partnership, the statement of preferred taxation scheme is submitted by all the partners or shareholders. The authority authorised to accept such a statement is the head of the tax office having jurisdiction over the place of residence of each of the partners or shareholders. Partners in a civil partnership of natural persons who start their business activity may submit a statement on the choice of lump-sum taxation of inventoried revenues pursuant to the provisions of the Act on Freedom of Economic Activity.

If a taxpayer fails to report the dissolution of their economic activity or fails to choose another form of taxation by 20 January of the fiscal year, they are assumed to continue their activity and continue to be subject to lump-sum taxation on inventoried revenues.

This form of taxation is not available to all taxpayers. Taxpayers who elect the fixed-rate tax scheme cannot use lump tax on inventoried revenues. In addition, the latter form of taxation is denied to those natural persons

---

78 S. Babiarz, S. Bogucki, A. Dumas, R. Pęk, S. Presnarowicz, J. Pustuł, *Ryczałty w prawie podatkowym*, LexisNexis, Warsaw 2012, pp. 59–89.

who, in the year preceding the fiscal year, earned revenues from their economic activity exceeding EUR 250,000. Likewise, lump tax on inventoried revenues is not available to taxpayers who raise revenues from the types of economic activity listed in the statute, e.g. pharmacies, pawnshops, foreign exchange offices, legal services, production of excised goods.

Taxable object is the taxpayer's revenue. Its value is, in principle, determined based on the revenue records kept by the taxpayer. Such records are required of taxpayers who earn revenues from a non-agricultural economic activity. Where a taxpayer does not keep revenue records or does it incorrectly, the tax authority is authorised to establish the value of the non-inventoried revenue and determine the lump sum tax on that value. Such a lump tax is a "penalty" levy as it represents five times the tax rate that would be applied to inventoried revenue. The provisions of the Act on Lump-Sum Income Tax on Selected Revenues Earned by Natural Persons read that the lump sum determined in the manner discussed above cannot be greater than 75% of the revenue.

The obligation of keeping revenue records does not apply to taxpayers who earn revenues only from lease or sublease, tenancy or subtenancy or other similar agreements if the amount of their revenue is given in the relevant written agreement.

Taxpayers are obliged to calculate the lump sum tax on inventoried revenues each month and pay it to the tax office's bank account by the 20th day of the following month (for December – by 31 January of the following year).

Taxpayers who did not earn more than the equivalent of EUR 25,000 in the year preceding the fiscal year may elect to handle their taxes over a longer settlement period. In such a case, the assessment and payment of the lump-sum tax on inventoried revenues to the tax office's bank account may take place by the 20th day of the month following the end of the taxable quarter. The payment of tax for the last quarter of the fiscal year should be effected by 31 January of the following year.

Each taxpayer liable to lump-sum tax on inventoried revenues is obliged to submit a tax return by 31 January of the year following the fiscal year. The tax return shows the size of earned revenue, allowable expenses and due lump-sum tax on inventoried revenues.

The amount of output tax is assessed on the basis of a fairly complex tax scale. **The rates** are given in percentage and vary, depending on the pursued economic activity, from 2% to 20%. For example, the 20% rate is applicable revenues earned in liberal professions, 8.5% is applicable to revenues from lease or tenancy, 2% is applicable to revenues from the sale of self-grown or self-bred plant and animal products processed in a manner other than industrial processing.

The statute provides for a number of exemptions. They apply, among others to:

a) revenues from the rental of guest rooms in residential buildings located in the rural area in an agricultural holding to persons on holiday; and revenues earned from catering services provided to such persons if the number of rented rooms is lower than five;

b) subsidies received from the state budget for the co-financing of specific action supporting agriculture and rural development;

c) amounts earned from interest received in connection with the refund of overpaid tax obligations and other budgetary receivables.

4.6.3 Lump Income Tax on the Revenues of the Clergy

Generally, the revenues of the members of the clergy are subject to taxation on general terms, i.e. as stipulated in the Natural Persons' Income Tax. Such a form of taxation required the clergy to keep a revenue and expense book.

An alternative solution is lump-sum income tax. To be liable to a lump-sum taxation scheme, a clergyman notifies the competent head of the tax office of the commencement of their pastoral duties within 14 days afterwards.

The level of the lump-sum tax depends on three factors:

1) performed pastoral function (parish priest, curate);
2) the population within the boundaries of the parish: as at 31 December of the year preceding the fiscal year;
3) the population of the municipality or town where the parish is located. This criterion is not applicable when establishing the lump-sum tax parish priests' revenue.

A disadvantage of this form of taxation is that when establishing the size of the lump-sum tax, it is the number of inhabitants of the parish that is taken into account and not the number of the faithful (actual churchgoers). This approach is somewhat mitigated by a solution which allows the reduction of tax – by the tax authority at the request of the clergyman concerned – if the number of the faithful in a specific denomination is no more than half of the parish population.

The head of the tax office having jurisdiction over the place of pastoral work issues a decision determining the amount of the lump-sum tax for the given fiscal year. The tax is paid on a quarterly basis without a reminder to the tax office's bank account by the 20th day of the month following the end of the quarter. The tax due for the last quarter of the year is paid by 28 December of the fiscal year. The output tax paid by the clergy may be reduced by the amount of the health insurance contribution. The amount of the health insurance contribution reducing the lump-sum tax cannot exceed 7.75% of the contribution assessment base.

The clergy may waive the lump-sum taxation scheme for a given fiscal year. The relevant notification should be submitted to the tax authority by 20 January of the fiscal year. Where a clergyman begins their pastoral function during the tax year, the waiver of a lump-sum taxation scheme should take place by the day preceding the day of commencement of this function.

Such taxpayers may benefit from the payment of income tax as a lump sum only on the revenue earned from fees received in connection with their pastoral functions. The revenues of the clergy obtained from other sources (e.g. contract of employment, contract of mandate) are taxed on general terms.

4.7 Tonnage Tax

Tonnage tax was introduced into the Polish taxation system on 1 January 2007.[79] It is another simplified form of taxation of income applicable to **shipping operators** operating merchant vessels in international shipping. According to the Act on Tonnage Tax, tonnage tax payers are: natural persons, legal persons, partnerships limited by shares and partners in

---

79 Act of 24 August 2006 on Tonnage Tax (Journal of Laws of 2018, item 381).

partnerships, unlimited partnerships, or limited partnerships if they have their registered office, management centre or domicile in the territory of the Republic of Poland. Moreover, a shipping operator can also be a foreign entrepreneur involved in an economic activity in the territory of the Republic of Poland subject to tonnage tax. Tonnage tax payers must meet one of the following conditions:

a) own a vessel;
b) perform, on their own behalf, sea navigation in their own or third-party's ship and hold the so-called Document of Compliance;
c) manage a third-party's ship under an agreement and hold the Document of Compliance.

It is the taxpayer themselves that decide to be burdened with tonnage tax. Once this taxation scheme is chosen, the taxpayer submits a relevant statement to the head of the tax office competent in income tax. The statement must be submitted by 20 January of the first fiscal year. If a shipping operator is commencing their business, this statement should be submitted before the commencement date. Once opting to be covered by the tonnage tax system, a shipping operator must uphold it for 10 years. The law does not provide for a change of the form of taxation over this period.

The taxable **object** in tonnage tax is the income earned by a shipping operator. For fiscal purposes, it is important to ensure that the services of international shipping be rendered with vessels with a gross tonnage of more than 100 GT each. At the same time, the law offers a list of specific services rendered by the shipping operator. They include salvage and cargo or passenger carriage services. In the latter case, when services are provided by a tugboat, the income of the shipping operator is subject to tonnage tax, provided that at least 50% of the actual annual working time is earmarked to the carriage of cargo or passengers by sea. The same requirement is imposed on taxpayers providing dredger services: at least 50% of the actual annual working time must be the carriage of the excavated material by sea.

A characteristic feature of tonnage tax is that it may also apply to income earned by a shipping operator from other pursued activities. It is necessary, however, that this additional activity is directly related to the provision of salvage or cargo or passenger carriage services. This may be, for example: the operation of passenger terminals, the sale of goods or services on board, the operation of foreign exchange offices on board, the leasing and use of containers or loading, unloading, and repair operations. The income from the following activities is tonnage tax-exempt: fishery or fish processing; construction of: seaports, wind turbines, transmission pipelines on the seabed, repair and development of port infrastructure or port facilities; waterways; dredging of waterways and water reservoirs; underwater works; geological exploration and extraction of mineral resources from the seabed; provision of pilot services within seaports; passenger transport within ports and marinas; operation of permanently anchored or moored vessels unfit for navigation; education, scientific research, sports, or recreational travel.

The tax base in tonnage tax is the shipping operator's income raised on the business activity. It is assessed as the product of the daily rate and the period of operation of all vessels owned by the shipping operator in a given month. The amount of the daily rate depends on the net tonnage of the vessel for every 100 units; the rates are given in EUR. The income so established is taxable at the rate of 19%.

Notwithstanding the above, the law provides for a special type of tax rate. It applies to the sale of vessels. Then, the tax rate is 15%. However, the application of this reduced rate of tonnage tax is contingent upon the fulfilment of another condition. Revenues earned from the sale of a ship are subject to a tonnage tax of 15% if a shipping operator, within three years from the date of sale, does not spend them on the acquisition of ownership or joint ownership, repair, upgrading, or conversion of ships.

Tonnage tax payers calculate the tax for each month of the fiscal year and pay it to the competent tax authority. The tax payments should be made by the 20th day of each month for the previous month and by 31 January for December of the previous year. Notwithstanding the above, the taxpayers are obliged to submit an annual tax return stating the amount of tonnage tax for the fiscal year. The return should be submitted to the tax office by 31 January of the following year.

Tonnage tax is a relatively new tax instrument in the Polish tax system. Upon its introduction, it was hoped that the new levy would translate into the development of maritime economy. These hopes have faded over time. Also, this tax has next to no fiscal significance for the state budget.[80]

4.8 Tax on Extraction of Selected Minerals

Tax on extraction of selected minerals was introduced in 2012.[81] It is collected next to numerous fees and charges that go with the mining business, such as the stamp duty for licences or operating fees that supply municipal budgets. This tax is also complementary to corporate and personal income tax, goods and services tax and excise tax that are inseparable from the economic activity.

Taxable are natural persons, legal persons and organisational units without legal personality that extract the following minerals as part of their economic activity:

a) copper;
b) silver;
c) natural gas;
d) crude oil.

The object of taxation has been subject to clear restrictions. The tax liability does not cover the production of copper ore in the volume below 1 tonne a month if used for research purposes. Tax-exempts are also the monthly extraction of small amounts of gas (11 MWh) and crude oil (1 tonne). Also, in such cases, these minerals are tax-free if earmarked for research purposes. Methane is not taxed and, exceptionally, the condition of using it for a research purpose is not applicable.

The **tax base** was established by determining the physical quantity of metals and the value of extracted hydrocarbons. Naturally, the assessment method will vary. It follows from the fact that the tax base for metals can be expressed in different weight parameters. It is kilograms for silver and

---

80 More about tonnage tax: M. Burzec, "*Podatek tonażowy*," [in:] *Prawo podatkowe*, eds. P. Smoleń, W. Wójtowicz, C.H. Beck, Warsaw 2017b, pp. 425–430; K. Wojewoda-Buraczyńska, "Zmiany w podatku tonażowym," *Przegląd Prawa publicznego* 2015, No. 3, pp. 74–83.

81 Act of 2 March 2012 on Tax on Extraction of Selected Minerals (Journal of Laws of 2018, item 228).

tonnes for copper. Moreover, the taxable amount for hydrocarbons is expressed in Polish zlotys (PLN). To determine the monetary value requires the data on the volume of extraction and the average price. An exception to this natural gas extraction as an associated mining product since the value of this extraction is the amount of the monthly revenue from its supply. The value of extracted crude oil is the product of the extracted volume given in tonnes and the average price of crude oil. The value of extracted natural gas is the product of the extracted volume given in megawatt hours (MWh) and the average price of natural gas. The values of both hydrocarbons are aggregated in the tax base if they are extracted together by the same taxpayer.

Applicable tax law does not fully regulate the average prices of hydrocarbons. Yet, it requires the Minister of Finance to announce – in the Journal of Laws by the 15th day of each month – the average price of one megawatt hour of natural gas and crude oil for the previous month in PLN and rounded up to PLN 1. In the case of natural gas, this parameter is determined based on the arithmetic mean of daily natural gas quotations (Day-Ahead Market) on Towarowa Giełda Energii S.A. (Polish Power Exchange – POLPX) in the previous month. On the other hand, the parameter for crude oil is based on the arithmetic mean of the average USD exchange rate announced by the National Bank of Poland in the previous month and the arithmetic mean of the daily crude oil quotations (OPEC daily basket price) established by the Organisation of the Petroleum Exporting Countries in the previous month and given in USD per barrel, rounded up to one cent.[82]

The differentiated tax base and the complex process of its determination directly affects the differentiation of tax rates. The law permits amount and percentage rates. Amount rates apply to the taxation of copper and silver. Percentage rates apply to natural gas and crude oil extraction.

The assessment of output tax is a demanding process, and the calculation of the amount due makes this tax stand out among other fiscal burdens. A characteristic feature is that the law fails to give the amount of tax per established tax assessment base explicitly but prescribes its detailed calculation. Determining the amount of tax liability requires separate assessment

---

82 M. Duda, "Podatek od wydobycia niektórych kopalin – nowa jakość w polskim prawie podatkowym," *Ruch Prawniczy Ekonomiczny i Socjologiczny* 2013, No. 1, pp. 121–123.

of partial tax amounts on the specific categories of minerals extracted and utilised for industrial purposes in order to sum these values up in the step of the tax assessment procedure. Such an approach complicates the assessment significantly.

The tax rate is variable since its calculation follows the so-called "metal indexation clause." It makes the tax burden dependent on the parameter of the average price of copper and silver. It is given as the PLN average monthly price of daily market quotations of 1 tonne of copper and 1 kilogram of silver. It takes account of the average USD/PLN exchange rate (announced by the central bank) and the arithmetic mean of the daily quotations of these metals on the London markets: London Metal Exchange (LME) for copper and London Bullion Market Association (LBMA) for silver. Both the exchange rate and the arithmetic mean of daily quotations include the data for the month preceding the month of tax assessment. The Minister of Finance calculates the tax parameter of the average price of copper and silver which is announced in the Journal of Laws by the 15th day of every month.

The calculation of the mine tax rate follows a number of statutory formulas. There are four of them. How the tax will be assessed depends on whether the threshold value of the average metal price is exceeded. This price is raised annually in proportion to the inflation growth of the goods and services price index. The impact of metal quotations on the amount of rate is limited by the introduction of statutory restrictions on the minimum and maximum rates. The maximum rate for copper is PLN 16,000 per tonne while for silver PLN 2,100 per kilogram. In contrast, the minimum rates are determined by the uniform standard of 0.5% compared against the average price of each of these metals.

The percentage rates are primarily differentiated by the type of hydrocarbon and the average permeability and average effective porosity of the extracted deposit. The applicable rates are 1.5%, 3%, and 6% depending on the type and location of the deposit.[83]

The taxpayer is obliged to prepare monthly tax returns, submit them to the competent head of the tax office and pay the tax to the 25th day of the following month for the previous month.

---

83 A. Gorgol, "*Podatek od wydobycia niektórych kopalin,*" [in:] *Prawo podatkowe*, eds. P. Smoleń, W. Wójtowicz, C.H. Beck, Warsaw 2017, pp. 437–438.

4.9 Special Hydrocarbon Tax

Special hydrocarbon tax to some extent supplements the tax on extraction of selected minerals, specifically in the part concerning natural gas and crude oil.[84]

The taxpayers of special hydrocarbon tax are entities engaged in the extraction of hydrocarbons. The scope of taxation applies both to natural persons, legal persons, and other organisational units. Civil partnership is also a taxpayer but not its partners.

The **taxable object** is the profit from the extraction of hydrocarbons. Hydrocarbon extraction activity is an activity of extracting hydrocarbons from deposits, including the prospecting for and exploration of hydrocarbon deposits, conducted in the territory of the Republic of Poland or in a territory outside territorial waters which is an exclusive economic zone. The activity commences on the day of obtaining a licence or reporting a geological project to the competent authority; it ends on the day of liquidation of the mining plant.

As follows from the statute, profit is the excess amount of revenues over the so-called eligible expenditure. At the same time, the statute sets a specific tax-free minimum. The amount of tax-free profit is expressed by the R-factor lower than the conversion factor of 1.5. According to the statutory definition, this parameter is the ratio of cumulative revenue to cumulative eligible expenditure. Eligible expenditure is deducted from the revenue from the extraction of hydrocarbons. This expenditure is incurred by the taxpayer in order to earn revenue or preserve or secure their revenues. They include expenditure incurred for the prospecting, exploration, extraction, storage or supply of extracted hydrocarbons and the termination of extraction of hydrocarbons and not returned to the taxpayer in any form. Besides these, the statute enumerates expenses that are deemed non-eligible.

The revenues are cash receipts, pecuniary values and the value of receivables paid in kind, including advances and prepayments, for the delivery of extracted hydrocarbons. Delivery is understood as transferring, in any form,

---

84 Act of 25 July 2014 on Special Hydrocarbon Tax (Journal of Laws of 2018, item 246).

the right to dispose of the extracted hydrocarbon as the owner will. The revenues are reduced by due VAT, refunds and prepayments.

The tax base is the profit from the extraction of hydrocarbons as an excess amount of the revenue earned in the given fiscal year on extraction over the eligible expenditure incurred in that year. The tax base is established for the fiscal year, which does not need to overlap with the calendar year.

The tax rates are given in percentage. Tax law differentiates these rates depending on the value of the R-factor. As a result, three tax rates are available. Two of them are established directly in the law: 0% and 25%. The zero rate applies when the R-factor is lower than 1.5. In contrast, the 25% rate is linked to this parameter when it is equal to or greater than 2. On the other hand, if it falls between 1.5 and 2, the third type of the special rate comes into play. Such a special rate should be calculated according to the statutory formula $(25 \times \text{R-factor} - 25)/100$. This mechanism complicates tax assessments significantly.

As with the tax on extraction of selected minerals, the taxpayer is obliged to submit monthly tax returns to the competent head of the tax office and pay the tax by the 25th day of the month. By the end of the third month of the following fiscal year, the taxpayer also submits an annual statement of the amount of profit (loss) in the fiscal year, cumulated revenues and cumulative eligible expenditure. At the same time, they pay to the tax office account the output tax or the difference between the output tax on the profit shown in the annual statement and the amount of tax advances due for the period from the beginning of the year.

4.10 Tax on Selected Financial Institutions

Tax on selected financial institutions is a new form of taxation in Poland. It was introduced in 2016 and covers selected types of financial institutions.[85] It is commonly known as **bank tax** as the key taxpayers are banks and cooperative savings and credit unions. In addition, it is levied on credit institutions offering consumer credits, insurance companies, and reinsurance

---

85 Tax on certain financial institutions was introduced in Poland by the Act of 15 January 2016 (Journal of Laws No. 68, as amended) which entered into force on 1 February 2016.

undertakings. Tax liable are the institutions having a registered place of business in Poland. As regards other financial institutions, the legislator levied the tax on the branches of foreign banks, branches of credit institutions and branches of foreign insurance and reinsurance companies. According to statute, state-owned banks are exempted from this tax. Temporary exemption is also available to those financial institutions that implement the so-called resolution.

The tax base is the excess amount of total assets over PLN 4 billion. Lower base thresholds for the establishment of the excess amount apply to credit institutions (PLN 200 million) and insurance and reinsurance companies (PLN 2 billion). The tax base can be reduced by the value of certain funds and assets acquired from the National Bank of Poland.

Tax on selected financial institutions is collected monthly at the same rate: 0.0366%. Taxpayers who submit tax returns calculate and pay the tax by the 25th day of the following month.

5 Taxes Intended for the Municipal Budget

5.1 Tax on Transactions under Civil Law

5.1.1 Taxable Object

The tax on transactions entered into under civil law[86] has been in force since 1 January 2001. It was isolated from the Act on Stamp Duty. Until 2000, the stamp duty had been imposed on the activities of administrative authorities, documents, and judicial decisions, on the one hand, and on performed civil law transactions, on the other.

The Act on Transactions under Civil Law contains a closed set of taxable activities (transactions). There are three categories of taxable objects. The **first category** comprises such acts in civil law as: contracts of sale and exchange of things and property rights; contracts of loan of money or things designated only as to their kind; contracts of donation – in the part relating to the donee taking over debts and burdens or obligations of the donor; contracts of annuity; contracts of division of inheritance and contracts of dissolution of co-ownership – in the part relating to repayments or additional payments; establishment of mortgage; establishment of usufruct for consideration, including irregular usufruct, and servitude for consideration; contracts of irregular deposit; deed of partnership (company). The **second category** includes amendments to the instruments named above if they lead to a higher tax base; the **third category** covers the pronouncements of courts, including conciliatory courts, and settlements if they produce the same legal effects as the taxable acts in civil law.

In addition, a territorial criterion has been introduced to the concept of tax on civil law transactions. This means that the transactions named in the statute are taxed if their object is:

a) things located in the territory of the Republic of Poland or property rights exercised in the territory of the Republic of Poland;

---

86 The Act of 9 September 2000 on Transactions under Civil Law (Journal of Laws of 2017, item 1150).

b)   things located abroad or property rights exercised abroad, in the case
where the acquirer has the place of residence or seat in the territory of
the Republic of Poland and the act in civil law was performed in the
territory of the Republic of Poland.

In the case of a contract of exchange, at least one of the things must be
located in the territory of Poland or one of the property rights must be exercised in the territory of Poland. On the other hand, a partnership (company)
deed and its amendments are subject to tax if, at the time of performing the
act in civil law, the seat of the partnership is in the territory of the Republic
of Poland or the actual management centre or the seat of the company is
in territory of the Republic of Poland.

Tax on civil law transactions (hereinafter "TCLT") corresponds to and
is complementary with value-added tax (VAT). Hence, many doubts as to
whether a given act in civil law should be burdened with VAT or TCLT. This
problem has been addressed by excluding from TCLT transactions (other
than a partnership (company) deed and its amendments) which are subject
to value added tax, also if at least one of the parties is VAT-exempt relative to the performed transaction. Exceptions to this rule are the contracts
of sale and exchange if they concern real property, its part or the right of
perpetual usufruct, cooperative member's ownership right to residential
premises, the right to a single-family dwelling in a housing cooperative or
the right to a parking space in a multi-vehicle garage or a share in those
rights. In such a situation, the contracts mentioned above, if not subject to
VAT, are always subject to TCLT.[87]

Some other activities excluded from TCLT are: acts in civil law concerning alimony, care, guardianship, and adoption, social insurance, health
insurance, science, education and extramural teaching and health; contracts
of sale and exchange of things that, within the meaning of customs law,
are goods: introduced into a duty-free zone; placed under the customs
warehousing procedure; partnership (company) deeds and their amendments connected with: company mergers, transformation of a company
into a different company, contribution to a company, in exchange for its

---

87 I. Krawczyk, "Podatek od czynności cywilnoprawnych a VAT," *Przegląd Podatkowy* 2001, No. 5, p. 33.

shares, of: company's enterprise or its organised part, shares of another company which give the majority of votes in it or additional shares in the case when the company to which these shares are contributed already holds the majority of votes.[88]

5.1.2 Tax Liability

The occurrence of tax liability depends on the type of taxed civil law transaction. As a rule, tax liability arises at the moment of conducting a civil law transaction. It may also arise: upon adoption of the resolution on increasing the capital of a company having legal personality; upon the filing of a declaration on the establishment of a mortgage or conclusion of a contract of establishment of a mortgage; upon making any disbursement of cash means, where a contract of loan sets forth that the disbursement of cash means shall be made more than once and the means total is not known at the moment of conclusion of the contract; upon the court pronouncement becoming valid, judgement of the conciliatory court being served or upon making a settlement.

5.1.3 Taxable Person

The taxable person in TCLT may be a natural person, a legal person or organisational unit without legal personality, provided that such entities appear in cash or unprofessional trading of things or property rights. In principle, the entity obliged to pay tax will be the person acquiring things or property rights. For example, the taxpayer in the case of contract of sale is the buyer; in the case of contract of donation – the donee; in the case of contract of annuity – the acquirer of ownership of immovable property; in the case of contract of loan – the borrower; in the case of establishment of a mortgage – the person making declaration of intent concerning the establishment of a mortgage; in the case of deed of a civil partnership – the partners, and in other partnership or company deeds – the partnership or

---

88 See more: H. Filipczyk, *Podatek od czynności cywilnoprawnych. Komentarz*, Wolters Kluwer, Warsaw 2015, 59 et seq.; D. Michta, L. Pankrac, *Ustawa o podatku od czynności cywilnoprawnych. Komentarz*, LexisNexis, Warsaw 2013, p. 11 et seq.

company; in the case of establishment of usufruct for consideration and servitude for consideration – the usufructuary or the party acquiring the right of servitude.

5.1.4 Tax Base and the Amount of Tax

The tax base in TCLT is, in principle, the market value determined based on the average prices reported on the day of transaction in the trading in things of the same kind and type, taking account of their location, condition and degree of wear, and in the trading in property rights of the same kind. This is the gross market value, free from debt and other burdens.

In some types of civil law transactions, the tax base can be: the value of debt and burdens (in contracts of donation); the value of benefits (in establishing usufruct for consideration or servitude for consideration); the amount or value of a loan (in contracts of loan); the value of contribution of share capital (in partnership or company deeds); the amount of secured liability (in establishing a mortgage).

The size of tax rates depends on the type of act in civil law. They are as follows:

- 0.1% – for the establishment of a mortgage (of the amount of secured liability);
- 0.5% – for a partnership or company deed;
- 1% – for contracts of establishing usufruct for consideration or servitude for consideration; for contracts of sale, exchange, annuity; division of an inheritance, dissolution of co-ownership, donation, and other property rights;
- 2% – for contracts of loan, sale, exchange, annuity, division of an inheritance, dissolution of co-ownership, donation, related to property ownership and related rights and to movables.

TCLT also provides for the 20% tax rate. It may be imposed in two cases. **First,** when the taxpayer refers to the fact of having concluded a contract of loan, irregular deposit or establishment of irregular usufruct or of having amended them, and the tax payable on such acts has not been paid. **Second,** when the person taking out a loan refers to the fact of having concluded a contract of loan with the spouse, descendant, ascendant, stepson, siblings, stepfather or stepmother, has not fulfilled the condition of documenting the receipt of money, for example, in a bank account.[89]

5.1.5 Tax Exemptions

TCLT offers exemptions falling both within the scope related to objects and persons. The persons entitled to the exemption are: municipalities, districts, provinces, the State Treasury, persons purchasing their own rehabilitation equipment, wheelchairs, scooters, motorcycles or motor cars, the Material Reserves Agency, public benefit organisations and, pursuant to the reciprocity principle, foreign states, their diplomatic representation offices and consular offices.

The exemptions as to the object cover, but not only: the sale of movables if the tax base does not exceed PLN 1,000; the sale of treasury bills and bonds; the sale of goods in commodity exchanges; real property sold for public purposes; exchange of a dwelling or its part and residential premises constituting a separate property if the parties are the immediate family; the sale of land being an agricultural holding, provided that, as a result of the transaction, a new holding is be established or an existing holding will be enlarged so that its area is no less than 11 ha and no more than 300 ha and that the farm is run by the purchased for the period of at least five years from the day of acquisition; loans granted by entrepreneurs not having their registered office or management centre in Poland and conducting a lending activity; cash loans under a contract of loan concluded between the closest family members of up to PLN 9,637; loans under a contract of loan concluded with other persons up to the total amount of PLN 5,000 from one party and up to PLN 25,000 from multiple parties – over the period of three consecutive calendar years.[90]

5.1.6 Tax Payment and Collection

A tax obligation related to TCLT arises *ex lege*. This means that taxpayers are obliged, without the request of the tax authority, to submit a tax statement, calculate tax and pay it within 14 days as of the occurrence of tax

---

89 R. Mastalski, *Prawo podatkowe*, C.H. Beck, Warsaw 2017a, pp. 609–610.
90 M. Gargul, W. Oleś, *Podatek od czynności cywilnoprawnych*, LexisNexis, Warsaw 2013, p. 180 et seq.

liability. This rule does not apply if this tax is collected by the tax remitter, i.e. the notary public (e.g. in cases of transfer of ownership of real property). This being the case, the notary is obliged to calculate, collect and pay the tax to the tax authority.

5.2 Inheritance and Gift Tax

5.2.1 Taxable Object

The taxation of gratuitous acquisition of property is regulated by the 1983 Act on Inheritance and Gift Tax.[91] The taxable object in inheritance and gift tax (hereinafter "IGT") is the acquisition of ownership of a property located in the territory of Poland or property rights exercised in the territory of Poland, pursuant to:

- succession, ordinary legacy, further legacy, special bequest, testamentary instruction;
- gift, donor's instruction;
- prescription[92];
- gratuitous dissolution of co-ownership;
- reserved share;
- gratuitous: annuity, use, or servitude.

IGT may also be levied on the acquisition of rights to a bank deposit based on the authorisation to dispose of the deposit *mortis causa* and the acquisition of units based on the authorisation of the participant in open funds *mortis causa*.

IGT also applies to the acquisition of property outside Poland or property rights exercised outside Poland if, at the time of the opening of the succession or conclusion of a gift contract, the acquiring party was a Polish citizen, or their domicile was in Poland. *A contrario*, IGT will not be levied on the acquisition of movable property located in Poland or property rights

---

91 Act of 28 July 1983 on Inheritance and Gift Tax (consolidated text: Journal of Laws of 2018, item 644 as amended).

92 In Poland prescription of movable property takes place after a continuous three-year holding in good faith; prescription of immovables (property, predial servitude, and servitude of passage) takes place after 20 years (in good faith) or after 30 years (in bad faith).

exercisable in the territory of Poland if, on the date of acquisition, neither the acquiring party nor the donor or testator were Polish citizens and had their domicile in Poland.

In addition, IGT is ruled out in: the acquisition by way of succession, special bequest or gift of copyright and related rights, rights to inventions, trademarks, industrial designs and receivables arising from the acquisition of these rights; acquisition by way of succession of funds from the employee pension scheme; acquisition by way of succession of funds gathered by the deceased in the open pension fund, on the individual retirement account and on the individual retirement security account.[93]

5.2.2 Taxable Person

The payers of IGT are only natural persons. They are divided into three tax groups that reflect the acquirer's personal affinity with the person from whom the property or property rights were acquired or inherited. **Group 1** includes the following immediate family members: spouse, descendants, ascendants, stepson, son-in-law, daughter-in-law, sibling, stepfather, stepmother, and parents-in-law. **Group 2** includes the following persons: descendants of the siblings, parents' siblings, descendants and spouses of stepchildren, spouses of siblings and siblings' spouses, spouses of spouses' siblings, spouses of other descendants. **Group 3** includes all other acquiring parties.[94]

Since 2007, tax exemptions have covered the acquisition of property or property rights by the spouse, descendants, ascendants, stepson, siblings, stepfather, and stepmother. In order to be eligible for the exemption, it is necessary to report the fact of acquisition of property or property rights to the competent tax authority within six months of the date of the tax liability arising. In the case of succession, such a report must be submitted within six months from the date of validation of the court decision confirming the acquisition of inheritance.

---

93 P. Smoleń, *"Podatek od spadków i darowizn,"* [in:] *Prawo podatkowe*, eds. P. Smoleń, W. Wójtowicz, C.H. Beck, Warsaw 2017, pp. 485–488.

94 J. Głuchowski, P. Smoleń, "Klasyfikacja podatników na gruncie ustawy o po-datku od spadków i darowizn," *Gdańskie Studia Prawnicze* 2006, No. XVI, pp. 323–345.

5.2.3 Tax Liability

Tax liability in IGT encumbers the party acquiring the ownership of property and property rights. Its emergence depends on the type of activity through which the taxpayer acquired the ownership of property and property rights. In the case of acquisition by inheritance, the liability arises upon the acceptance of an inheritance. In contrast, acquisition by way of gift causes tax liability at the time the donor submits the relevant statement in the form of a notarial deed and, in the case of a contract concluded without the form provided – at the time of fulfilling the promised performance. In addition, tax liability may arise in the following cases (but not only):

- upon acquisition by way of prescription – when the decision of the court approving prescription becomes valid;
- upon acquisition of co-ownership by way of gratuitous dissolution – at the time of the conclusion of the relevant agreement or when the court's decision becomes valid;
- upon acquisition by way of gratuitous servitude, annuity or use – when these rights become acknowledged.

5.2.4 Exemptions from Inheritance and Gift Tax

IGT offers several exemptions that fall within three groups. The first group includes **exemptions related to housing**. They include, among other things: the gifts of money or other things by a person assigned to tax group 1 where the gift does not exceed the value of PLN 9,637 from one donor and the total of PLN 19,274 from multiple donors over five years from the date of the first gift, unless the acquired funds or things are spent or used – within 12 months – (i) for a construction or housing contribution to a housing co-operative, (ii) for the purchase of an apartment or construction of a house, (iii) for the repayment of a mortgage loan; (iv) for the acquisition by way of succession of the right to the contribution made to a housing cooperative by a person assigned to tax group 1 or 2.

The second group is made up of **assets acquired by farmers gratuitously**. These assets can be both movable and immovable property. Tax-exempt are also agricultural vehicles, agricultural machinery and spare parts for this equipment if they are not sold or gifted within three years as of the receipt. In addition, tax-exempt is the acquisition of agricultural land, provided that, as a result of the acquisition, an enlarged agricultural holding is established, its area being not smaller than 11 hectares and not greater than 300 hectares. Moreover, the acquiring party needs to assume the obligation of running the holding for at least five years. Exemption is also awarded to the acquisition of rights to contributions in an agricultural production cooperative or machinery rings.

The third groups of exemptions comprises the acquisition by way of inheritance or special bequest of items **of family and personal nature,** such as: home furnishings, bed linen, clothing, underwear and tools used in the household (where the acquiring parties are the persons assigned to tax groups 1 and 2); works of art and manuscripts produced by the testator and library materials if the testator was engaged in creative, scientific, educational, artistic, literary, or journalistic activities; movable historic monuments and collections entered in the register of monuments as well as items of historic value lent to the museum for scientific or exhibition purposes for a period not shorter than two years; acquisition by persons assigned to tax groups 1 and 2 of property entered in the register of monuments.[95]

5.2.5 Tax Base

The tax base in IGT is the value of acquired property and property rights less debt and encumbrances (including, for example, the costs of treatment and care during the last heir's illness, the cost of testator's burning ceremony and gravestone if paid from the testator's estate). In the case of acquisition by way of prescription, the value of expenses incurred by the acquiring party over the pre-prescription period is excluded from the tax base. In addition, excluded from the tax base are also the value of the building if it constitutes a part of the acquired land if it has been built by the person acquiring the property by way of prescription.

The value of acquired property and property rights is accepted in the amount determined by the purchaser as long as it is consistent with the market value.

---

95 J. Zdanowicz, "Zwolnienia w podatku od spadków i darowizn," *Monitor Podatkowy* 1999, No. 12, p. 12 et seq.

The concept of IGT offers a tax-free amount. Its amount depends of the acquirer's assignment to one of the tax groups. For taxpayers assigned to group 1, the tax-free amount is PLN 9,637. For taxpayers falling under groups 2 and 3, the tax-free amount is PLN 7,276 and 4,902, respectively.

5.2.6 Tax Rates

The size of tax rates depends on how things and property rights have been acquired. In the case of prescription, a flat-rate tax of 7% of the tax base is applied. In the remaining cases, the size of tax rates depends on the tax group that the acquiring party is assigned to. The tax is calculated according to the following scales:

Excess amount in PLN		The tax is
Over	To	
1) on acquirers assigned to the 1st tax group		
	10,278	3%
10,278	20,556	PLN 308.30 and 5% of excess amount over PLN 10,278
20,556		PLN 822.20 and 7% of excess amount over PLN 20,556
2) on acquirers assigned to the 2nd tax group		
	10,278	7%
10,278	20,556	PLN 719.50 and 9% of excess amount over PLN 10,278
20,556		PLN 1,644.50 and 12% of excess amount over PLN 20,556
3) on acquirers assigned to the 3rd tax group		
	10,278	12%
10,278	20,556	PLN 1,233.40 and 16% of excess amount over PLN 10,278
20,556		PLN 2,877.20 and 20% of excess amount over PLN 20,556

In addition, IGT has a special 20% rate. It applies when the taxpayer, in the course of tax proceedings, tax inspections or investigation, makes reference, before the tax authority, to the fact of having bestowed the gift but the tax due on this transaction has not been paid.

5.2.7 Housing Relief

Having fulfilled the requirements set forth in the law, the payers of IGT may take advantage of a housing relief. It is applicable in the acquisition of ownership of a building property or residential premises, a cooperative member's right to premises, a cooperative right to a single-family dwelling. The relief consists in the exclusion from the tax base of the value of the acquired property equivalent to no more than 110 m² of the property area. In the case of acquiring entities assigned to tax group 1, the relief is available to persons who have acquired the property right based on the gratuitous act *mortis causa* and *inter vivos*. On the other hand, in the case of persons assigned to tax groups 2 and 3, the relief may be obtained only by those who acquire the property only *mortis causa*. In addition, the heirs included in tax group 3 in order to benefit from the relief would have had to take care of the testator for at least two years pursuant to a contract made in writing with a notarised signature.

Moreover, the seeking of housing relief is possible when two conditions are met cumulatively. **First**, the person using the relief may not own another building or residential premises; may not hold a cooperative member's right to premises nor may be the owner of the cooperative ownership right to premises, the tenant of a building or residential premise. If the person holds one of the above rights, then within six months from the date of submission of their tax return, he or she should assign such a right to the descendants, the State Treasury or the municipality and, if they are a tenant, terminate the tenancy agreement. **Second**, the taxpayer is obliged to reside and be registered for permanent residence in the acquired property for at least five years from the date of submission of their tax return or conclusion of the contract of gift, or residence confirmed by the registration for permanent residence in the purchased building or residential premises.[96]

5.2.8 Payment Terms

The taxpayers are required to submit to the tax return to the competent head of the tax office within one month from the date on which the tax

---

96 More: P. Smoleń, *Kształtowanie obciążenia w podatku od spadków i darowizn*, Wydawnictwo KUL, Lublin 2006, p. 190 et seq.

liability arises. Based on the return, the tax authority issues a tax decision stating the amount of tax. The situation is different when the tax is collected by the tax remitter, i.e. the notary public. In such a case, the tax is calculated, collected and paid to the competent tax authority by the notary. This situation applies to the following acts done in the form of a notarial deed: gifts, contracts of gratuitous dissolution of co-ownership, contracts of gratuitous establishment of servitude and contracts of gratuitous establishment of usufruct.

5.3 Fixed-Rate Tax

Fixed-rate tax scheme is a lump-sum type of tax.[97] Its concept consists in the taxing of economic activity as such. In other words, the amount of taxpayers' revenue/income is irrelevant for the determination of the amount of due tax. The unique attribute of the fixed-rate tax scheme is that the amount of tax does not depend on the amount of income but on the type of business and the scale of this business conducted in a specific location. Flat-rate tax can be paid by taxpayers who perform an activity strictly defined in the law, such as: trade activity (e.g. trading in flowers, tobacco, beverages, foodstuffs), provision of certain services or manufacturing (e.g. car parking services, craft services, such as locksmith, hairdresser or beautician), catering, transport services (including passenger taxi services, hackney coach carriage, rickshaw carriage), entertainment services (e.g. operation of fairgrounds), home catering services, liberal professions (only veterinary and health care services provided by surgeons, physicians, dental technicians, nurses), educational services (e.g. one-to-one classes), care services (e.g. home care for children and the elderly), farming activities (e.g. services of carriage of milk, sale of sand, gravel, or peat from an agricultural holding, folkcraft).

The option of flat-rate tax is available to those taxpayers who submit, no later than by 20 January of the fiscal year, a request to be taxed by this method and in the request declare an economic activity for which the flat-tax rate scheme may be applied. Their economic activity must be conducted

---

97 P. Smoleń, *"Podatki samorządowe,"* [in:] *Prawo podatkowe – część ogólna i szczegółowa*, ed. W. Wójtowicz, C.H. Beck, Warsaw 2009, p. 343 et seq.

in the territory of Poland and may not involve the manufacture of excised goods. In addition, in their economic activity, the taxpayer may not benefit from the services of persons who are not employed by them under a contract of employment and from the services of other enterprises or establishments, unless they furnish specialised services. Besides, flat-rate taxpayers may not engage in other non-agricultural economic operation. Also, in order to take advantage of the flat-rate tax solution, the taxpayer's spouse may not take up a similar business activity.

Once meeting the requirements listed above, the head of the tax office, having examined the request of the would-be flat-rate taxpayer, issues a decision determining the amount of income tax payable in the form of flat-rate tax, separately for each fiscal year.

The size of the flat-rate tax, besides the type of pursued business, is also influenced by the population in the place of business and the extent of the activity itself manifested in the number of employees or its intensity, i.e. the number of working hours per month.

Flat-rate tax is paid as a specific amount and not percentage. Some taxpayers are entitled to **reduced rates**. For example, taxpayers who, by 1 January of the fiscal year, have turned 60 or have a low degree of disability officially acknowledged can expect a rate reduced by 20%. On the other hand, taxpayers who employ workers who have a low degree of disability officially acknowledged under separate regulations can obtain a reduction by 10% per each such employed person. Finally, taxpayers who, while being employed under a full-time contract of employment, provide services and do not employ contract and do not employ other people can enjoy a tax rate reduction by as much as 80%. Still, such taxpayers may not benefit from the remaining reductions. The head of the tax office may also reduce the tax rate at the taxpayer's request. This happens when the size of the taxpayer's business indicates that the original rate would be undoubtedly too high.[98]

The flat-rate tax scheme envisages not only decreased but also increased rates. Rate increases occur when the taxpayer employs, in their services or manufacturing business (except for the service of car parking lots), full

---

98 J. Małecki, "*Państwowe podatki bezpośrednie*," [in:] *Podatki i prawo podatkowe*, eds. A. Gomułowicz, J. Małecki, LexisNexis, Warsaw 2010a, p. 670.

age family members (excluding the spouse) and, in the case of transport services, also the full age members of one of the partner's family (excluding the spouse) and personnel employed solely for the sale of goods, receipt of service orders, maintenance activities, cash and accounts keeping, drivers and escorts, provided that the taxpayer has determined the scope of such employees' activities in writing. The rate increase is between 10% and 40% depending on the number of persons employed.

The payers of flat-rate tax are obliged to pay the levy by the seventh day of each month for the previous month. In December, the due tax is paid until 28 December. The due tax is reduced by the amount of contributions to the public health insurance. The deduction cannot be higher than 7.75% of the basis of the contribution.

After the end of the fiscal year, by 31 January, the taxpayer is required to submit to the competent tax authority an annual statement of the contributions paid and deducted in individual months.

5.4 Real Property Tax

5.4.1 Taxable Person

Real property tax is regulated by the provisions of the Act on Local Taxes and Fees.[99]

Taxpayers are natural persons, legal persons, and organisational units, including companies and partnerships without legal personality which are:

a) the owners of real property or construction structure (if owners–possessors – then the tax burden is incurred by the owner–possessor);
b) the owners of real property or construction structure;
c) the perpetual usufructuaries of land;
d) the possessors of real property or its parts or construction structure owned by a local self-government unit or the State Treasury if the possession is provided under a contract or has no legal title.[100]

---

99   Act on 12 January 1991 on Local Taxes and Fees (consolidated text: Journal of Laws of 2017, item 1785 as amended).
100 B. Pahl, *Podatki i opłaty lokalne. Teoria i Praktyka*, Wolters Kluwer, Warsaw 2017, pp. 68–84.

Where real property or construction structure are co-owned or possessed by two or more entities, the emerging tax liability shall be jointly and severally incurred by all the co-owners or possessors.

5.4.2 Taxable Object

The taxable objects in real property tax are the following types of real property or construction structure:

a) land;
b) buildings or their parts;
c) building structures[101] or their parts connected with the conducted economic activity.

Real property tax is not levied on arable land and forests, unless they are used for commercial purposes. Arable land and forests are excluded from taxation because they are subject to agricultural and forest taxes. Property excluded from tax are also: land occupied by the road strips of public roads; land under running surface water (except for land under lakes or artificial reservoirs); land under the inland maritime waters.

In addition, real property tax is not imposed on real property or its parts occupied by the local self-government bodies, including municipal offices, district administration, metropolitan union offices, and provincial offices.

On the reciprocity basis, excluded from tax is also property owned by foreign states or international organizations or handed over to them for perpetual usufruct; likewise, real property occupied by diplomatic missions, consular offices and other missions enjoying privileges and immunities provided for in applicable laws, agreements or customary international law.[102]

---

101 A structure is a construction structure within the meaning of the Building Law other than a small-architecture facilities (chapels, roadside crosses, statues, sandpits, swings, ladders, refuse stores, or garden architecture items) and other than a building. In Poland, structures are ski lifts, parking lots, power lines, windmills, free-standing advertising installations and advertising boards permanently fixed to the ground, pipelines, telecommunications lines, excavated holes, sports facilities. See: W. Krok, *Budowla w podatku od nieruchomości*, Wolters Kluwer, Warsaw 2010, p. 43 et seq.

102 L. Etel, *Podatek od nieruchomości. Komentarz*, Wolters Kluwer, Warsaw 2012, p. 89 et seq.

5.4.3 Exemptions from Real Property Tax

The real property exempt from tax includes, among others: land, buildings and structures of the railway infrastructure; seaport building infrastructure, building infrastructure enabling access to seaports and marinas and the land occupied by them; buildings and structures and the land occupied by them in the public use aerodromes; farm buildings or their parts used for the forestry, fishing, and agricultural activities, and for the special sections of agricultural production; land and buildings entered individually into the register of monuments, except for their parts occupied for economic activities; universities; public and private organisational units belonging to the education system (e.g. schools, kindergartens, psychological and pedagogical clinics); scientific institutes of the Polish Academy of Sciences; research institutes; entrepreneurs with the status of an R&D centre.[103]

Regardless of the list of exemptions contained in the statute, the municipal council may opt for other allowances within the scope related to objects of taxation.

5.4.4 Tax Base and Tax Rates

The tax base in real property tax depends on the type of taxable object. The object of taxation may be:

- for land – **the area** given in **square metres** or **hectares** confirmed in the register of land and buildings;
- for buildings or their parts – **useful floor area** given in square metres;
- for building structures or their parts connected with the pursued economic activity – **depreciation value**, as at 1 January of the fiscal year, underlying the calculation of depreciation in that year, not reduced by depreciation write-offs, and in the case of fully depreciated structures – their **value** as at 1 January of the years in which the last depreciation write-off took place.

The concept of real property tax envisages two types of tax rates: **percentage-** and **amount-based**. Structures are tax by the percentage rate. It is 2%

---

103 More: B. Janiak, "*Podatek od nieruchomości*," [in:] *Opodatkowanie nieruchomości*, eds. T. Kosieradzki, R. Piekarz, B. Janiak, Wolters Kluwer, Warsaw 2016, pp. 316–320.

of the structure value. On the other hand, specific amounts of tax are levied on land and buildings or their parts. In addition, the amount-based rates are differentiated depending on the use of the object of taxation. The top rates are paid for land and buildings or their parts used for a commercial activity.

The municipal council determines the amounts of tax rate in a resolution. However, these amounts cannot exceed the upper limits set out in the Act on Local Taxes and Fees. For example, the maximum annual rates in 2018 for 1 m^2 of usable floor space of buildings or their parts are: for residential premises – PLN 0.77; for premises related to economic activity – PLN 23.10; for premises related to the provision of healthcare services – PLN 4.70; for premises used for the economic activity of trading in certified seed – PLN 10.80; for other premises – PLN 7.77. When it comes to land related to the conducting of economic activity, the rates are: PLN 0.91 per 1 m^2; under standing or flowing surface waters such as lakes and reservoirs – PLN 4.63 per 1 ha; for other types of land – PLN 0.48 per 1 m^2. In addition, the municipal council may diversify the tax amounts according to such criteria as location, type of economic activity, type of structure, purpose and method of land use, technical condition, or the age of buildings.

5.4.5 Payment Terms and Procedure

According to the general rule, the tax liability in real property tax arises from the first day of the month following the month in which the circumstances occurred justifying the liability. Such circumstances may be, e.g. the purchase of real property or modification of records in the register of land and buildings. On the other hand, if the circumstance giving rise to tax liability is the existence of a building or its part, then the tax liability arises from 1 January of the year following the year of completed construction or first use of the building or structure, or their parts, before the final finishing works.

As regards natural persons, the tax liability in real property tax arises upon the service of the decision establishing the amount of tax obligation. Before that, such persons are obliged to submit to the competent tax authority the information on the real property – on a dedicated form and within 14 days of the occurrence of the circumstances justifying the liability. The amount of tax is established by the mayor having jurisdiction over the real property. The tax is payable in four proportional instalments to the following deadlines: 15 March, 15 May, 15 September, and 15 November of the fiscal year.

In relation to entities other than natural persons, the tax liability in real property tax is established by the law. As a result, legal persons, organisational units and companies or partnerships without legal personality are obliged to submit to the tax authority, by 31 January, a tax return and pay real property tax in instalments, proportional to the duration of the tax liability, for individual months up to the 15th day of each month and for January – until 31 January.

5.5 Agricultural Tax

5.5.1 Taxable Person

Agricultural tax is second oldest tax in Poland next to inheritance and gift tax. It was introduced by the Act of 15 November 1984 on Agricultural Tax.[104]

Agricultural taxpayers are natural persons, legal persons and organisational units, including companies and partnerships without legal personality which are:

- the owners of land (if owners–possessors – then the tax burden is incurred by the owner–possessor);
- the owners–possessors of land;
- the perpetual usufructuaries of land;
- the possessors of land owned by the local self-government units or the State Treasury if its possession is governed by a contract concluded with the owner, the Agricultural Property Agency or results from another legal title, or when there is no legal title to the possession.

The provisions of the Agricultural Tax Act also point to other taxable entities. They can be, but not only: a production cooperative (if the farm land has been contributed to the cooperative); a lessee if the farm land has been wholly or partially leased under a contract concluded pursuant to the farmers' social insurance regulations or regulations on structural pensions.

---

104 Act of 15 November 1984 on Agricultural Tax (consolidated text: Journal of Laws of 2017, item 1892).

The State Treasury and the municipality are released from the obligation to pay agricultural tax.

5.5.2 Taxable Object

Taxed with agricultural tax is land classified in the registry of land and buildings as agricultural land. In Poland, agricultural land includes: arable land, permanent meadows, permanent pastures, land under ponds, orchards that can be set up on arable land, permanent meadows, or permanent pastures.

Taxable with agricultural tax is not land classified in the registry of land and buildings as agricultural land that is occupied for an economic activity other than agricultural activity. The provisions of the Agricultural Tax Act define the agricultural activity as plant and animal production, including the production of seed, nursery material, breeding and reproduction material, vegetable production, ornamental plants, cultivated mushrooms, horticulture, breeding and production of animal seed material, birds and insects, animal farm production and fish farming.

5.5.3 Exemptions from Agricultural Tax

The concept of agricultural tax provides for several exemptions that are relevant both to the scope related to the object of taxation and to the taxpayer. Exempt from agricultural tax are, for example, utilised agricultural areas in classes V, VI, and VI; arable land, meadows and pastures under land melioration (the exemption applies only in the year in which such work actually took place); land of agricultural holdings created from the management of wasteland (the exemption is held for five years); land of agricultural holdings received by exchange or consolidation (the exemption is held for one year); land of agricultural holdings where agricultural production has been discontinued (the exemption is held no more than three years); land entered in the register of monuments; land intended for the establishment of a new holding or extension of an existing holding up to the area of 100 ha (the exemption is held for five years); universities; research institutes; scientific institutes and auxiliary units of the Polish Academy of Sciences; public and private schools; entrepreneurs with the status of an research and development centre.

5.5.4 Tax Base and Tax Rates

The tax base in agricultural tax depends on whether the land classified in the register of land and buildings as agricultural land forms or does not form part of the agricultural holding.

For the purposes of agricultural tax, the agricultural holding is defined as an area of land classified in the register of land and buildings as agricultural land of the total area of more than 1 ha or 1 conversion hectare, owned or possessed by a natural person, legal person or an organisational unit, including a partnership or company without legal personality.[105]

For land which is not part of the agricultural holding, the tax base is the **area given in physical hectares** as indicated in the register of land and buildings.

As regards the land of agricultural holdings, the tax base is the **area given in conversion hectares**. The conversion hectare is a unit created for agricultural tax purposes which represents the average revenue (gross income) earned from 1 ha of land. The number of conversion hectares is decided based on three criteria:

- the type of agricultural land (there are two of them: arable land and meadows and pastures);
- quality class of agricultural land (eight classes for arable land and six classes for meadows and pastures);
- participation of a given municipality or town in one the four tax regions (a key criterion of being assigned to a specific tax region is similar economic, climatic, and manufacture conditions).

---

105 Z. Czajka, *"Pojęcie gospodarstwa rolnego na gruncie przepisów prawa podatkowego. Wybrane zagadnienia,"* [in:] *Pobór podatków samorządowych,* ed. A. Krukowski, Wydawnictwo KUL, Lublin 2011, p. 99–126.

The table illustrating the conversion of agricultural areas

Types of agricultural areas:	Arable land				Meadows and pastures			
Tax regions	I	II	III	IV	I	II	III	IV
Classes of agricultural areas:	Conversion							
I	1.95	1.80	1.65	1.45	1.75	1.60	1.45	1.35
II	1.80	1.65	1.50	1.35	1.45	1.35	1.25	1.10
IIIa	1.65	1.50	1.40	1.25				
III					1.25	1.15	1.05	0.95
IIIb	1.35	1.25	1.15	1.00				
Iva	1.10	1.00	0.90	0.80				
IV					0.75	0.70	0.60	0.55
IVb	0.80	0.75	0.65	0.60				
V	0.35	0.30	0.25	0.20	0.20	0.20	0.15	0.15
VI	0.20	0.15	0.10	0.05	0.15	0.15	0.10	0.05

Orchard land is converted into conversion hectares according to the rules governing arable land. A separate method is used for the conversion of land under fish ponds. 1 ha of land under a pond stocked with salmon, bull trout, huchen, lake trout corresponds to 1 conversion hectare. On the other hand, 1 ha of land under a pond stocked with other species of fish is the equivalent of 0.20 conversion hectares. In the case of land under fishless ponds, physical hectares are converted according to the general rules applicable.

Agriculture tax rate is expressed as a specific amount. In the case of land forming part of agricultural holdings, the rate for 1 conversion ha is the cash equivalent of 250 kg of rye, calculated according to the average purchase price for 11 quarters preceding the quarter preceding the fiscal year. For the remaining types of land, the rate for 1 physical hectare is the cash equivalent of 500 kg of rye.

The average purchase price is determined based on the announcement of the President of the Central Statistical Office published in the *Monitor Polski*, the Journal of Laws of the Republic of Poland within 20 days after the end of the third quarter.

The municipal council is authorised to lower, by way of a resolution, the purchase price of rye underlying the calculation of agricultural tax in the municipality.

5.5.5 Reliefs in Agricultural Tax

The idea of agricultural tax allows for four reliefs.

One of them is an **investment relief**. Taxpayers who qualify for this relief have incurred expenditure on: construction or upgrading of buildings intended for animal husbandry and maintenance of farm animals and facilities serving environmental production; the purchase and installation of: a sprinkler system, rainy; water supply and agricultural hydraulics systems; equipment for the conversion of natural sources of energy for farming purposes (wind, biogas, sun, moving waters).

Under the investment relief, the taxpayer may deduct 25% of substantiated investment outlays from the output agricultural tax on land located within the municipality where the investment was held. This relief cannot continue for more than 15 years.

In localities located **in the piedmont or mountain areas**, i.e. where at least 50% of agricultural land is located above 350 m a.s.l., the co-called adjustment allowance can be sought. In this allowance, the level of agricultural tax for land classes I, II, IIIa, III, and IIIb is reduced by 30% and for land classes IVa, IV, and IVb by 60%.

Agricultural tax also provides for a **natural disaster relief**. The tax authority may grant a relief to the taxpayer who has suffered because of the official announcement of the state of natural disaster, as referred to in the Act of 18 April 2002 on the State of Natural Disaster. Granting a relief due to the state of natural disaster means that the authority may refrain from establishing the amount of tax or collecting tax in whole or in part. The size of relief depends on the extent of losses caused by the natural disaster to the holding. This type of relief is granted at the request of the taxpayer and for the fiscal year in which the disaster occurred. If a natural disaster occurs after the tax for a given fiscal year has been paid, then the taxpayer may qualify for the relief in the following fiscal year.[106]

The last relief in agricultural tax offers the taxpayer the opportunity to reduce the output tax **on account of the establishment of a new or extension of an existing agricultural holding up to area less than 100 hectares.** This relief can be applied after a five-year period of exemption from agricultural tax of agricultural land that creates or extends an existing agricultural holding. In the first year after the expiry of the five-year exemption period, the taxpayer is entitled to lower the output agricultural tax by 75% and by 50% in the second year.

It should be stressed that the municipal council may, by way of a resolution, set up other reliefs and allowances pertaining to the object of taxation.

5.5.6 Payment Terms and Procedure

The tax liability in agricultural tax arises from the first day of the month following the month in which the circumstances occurred justifying the liability (e.g. acquisition of land).

As regards natural persons, the tax liability in agricultural tax arises upon the service of the decision establishing the amount of tax. The amount of tax is established by the mayor having jurisdiction over the location of the land. The tax is payable in four proportional instalments to the following deadlines: 15 March, 15 May, 15 September, and 15 November of the fiscal year.

In the case of legal persons and organisational units, including partnerships and companies without legal personality, the tax liability in agricultural tax is established by law. The entities named above are obliged to submit, by 15 January, a tax return and pay the tax in instalments, proportional to the duration of the agricultural tax liability, to the following deadlines: 15 March, 15 May, 15 September, and 15 November.

---

106 M. Burzec, "*Opodatkowanie nieruchomości*," [in:] *Prawo podatkowe*, eds. P. Smoleń, W. Wójtowicz, C.H. Beck, Warsaw 2017a, pp. 473–475.

5.6 Forest Tax

5.6.1 Taxable Object

Forest tax was introduced into the Polish tax system in 1992. Before that, woodland had been regarded as part of an agricultural holding and had been subject to agricultural taxation. Today, forest tax is regulated by the Forest Tax Act.[107]

The object of taxation is forests, unless occupied for an economic activity other than forestry. According to the Forest Tax Act, forests are wooded areas classified in the register of land and buildings as forests.[108]

5.6.2 Taxable Person

Forest taxpayers are natural persons, legal persons and organisational units, including companies and partnerships without legal personality which are:

– the owners of forests;
– the owners–possessors of forests;
– the perpetual usufructuaries of forests;
– the possessors of forests owned by the State Treasury or local self-government units.

Where a forest is co-owned or possessed by two or more entities, tax liability shall be jointly and severally incurred by all the co-owners or possessors.

5.6.3 Tax Base and Tax Rates

The tax base in forest tax is the area of the forest given in hectares and confirmed in the register of land and buildings.

The tax rate on 1 ha for the fiscal year is the cash equivalent of 0.220 m³ of wood. The tax rate is calculated based on the average wood selling price, determined pursuant to the announcement by the President of the Central

---

107 Act of 30 October 2002 on Forest Tax (consolidated text: Journal of Laws of 2017, item 1821).
108 L. Etel, "*Podatki przychodowo-dochodowo-majątkowe*," [in:] *System prawa finansowego. Prawo daninowe*, ed. L. Etel, Wolters Kluwer, Warsaw 2010, p. 315 et seq.; R. Mastalski, *Prawo podatkowe*, C.H. Beck, Warsaw 2017a, pp. 637–638.

Statistical Office, obtained by forest districts for the first three quarters of the year preceding the fiscal year. The price of wood established based on the announcement of the President of the Central Statistical Office may be reduced by way of a resolution of the municipal council.

Due to the constraints associated with good forest management, the forest tax rate is subject to a statutory reduction of 50% in forests making up nature reserves and national parks.[109]

5.6.4 Exemptions from Forest Tax

Forest tax exemptions cover, but not only: forests with the growing stock up to 40 years of age; forests entered individually into the register of monuments; ecological utilised land; universities; scientific institutes of the Polish Academy of Sciences; research institutes.

Besides statutory exemptions, the municipal council may, by way of a resolution, allow exemptions in respect of the object of taxation.

5.6.5 Payment Terms and Procedure

The tax liability in forest tax arises from the first day of the month following the month in which the circumstances occurred justifying the liability (e.g. acquisition of forest).

As regards natural persons, the tax liability in forest tax arises upon the service of the decision establishing the amount of tax obligation by the mayor. The tax is payable in instalments proportional to the period of tax liability to the following deadlines: 15 March, 15 May, 15 September, and 15 November of the fiscal year.

In the case of legal persons and organisational units without legal personality, the tax liability in forest tax is established by law. Such entities are obliged to submit, by January 15, a tax return and pay the tax in instalments, proportional to the duration of the tax liability, for individual months until the 15th day of each month.

---

109 P. Borszowski, "*Podatek leśny,*" [in:] *Podatki i opłaty lokalne. Podatek rolny. Podatek leśny. Komentarz*, eds. P. Borszowski, K. Stelmaszczyk, Wolters Kluwer, Warsaw 2016, pp. 512–519.

5.7 Transportation Tax

This tax has been regulated by the provisions of the Act on Local Taxes and Fees. From 1 January 1998, tax on the means of transportation has been levied on the means of transport used for economic activities.[110]

The statute enumerates taxable means of transport such as:

- heavy goods vehicles of a maximum permissible laden weight above 3.5 t;
- tractors for semitrailers and ballast tractors adapted for use together with a trailer or semitrailer of a maximum permissible laden weight above 3.5 t;
- trailers and semitrailers which, together with a power-driven vehicle, have a maximum permissible laden weight of more than 7 t (tax-exempt are trailers and semitrailers related only to the agricultural activities conducted by the payer of agricultural tax);
- coaches.

The tax liability in tax on means of transport burdens natural persons and legal persons who own motor vehicles. When the tax liability arises depends on how the means of transport has been acquired. If the vehicle is registered in Poland for the first time, the tax liability arises as from the first day of month following the month of registration. On the other hand, if the acquired vehicle is already registered, the tax liability arises from the first day of the month following the month of acquisition.

The tax liability in tax on means of transport is established *ex lege*. The taxpayers are obliged to submit, by 15 February, a tax return to the competent tax authority: the mayor and pay the tax to the municipality's bank account. The tax is payable in two proportionate instalments over the duration of the tax liability by 15 February and 15 September each year.

The amount of tax is established annually in a resolution of the municipal council; however, it may not be higher than the maximum rates laid down in the Act on Local Taxes and Fees. The tax rates vary depending on the means of transport.

---

110 P. Smoleń, "*Podatki majątkowe,*" [in:] *System prawa finansowego. Prawo daninowe,* ed. L. Etel, Wolters Kluwer, Warsaw 2010, pp. 338–339.

Exempted from tax on means of transport are: vintage vehicles; means of transport constituting mobilisation rolling stock, special vehicles (excavators, sanders, snow ploughs, ambulances) and special purpose vehicles; and, on a reciprocity basis, the means of transport held by diplomatic missions, consular offices and other foreign missions enjoying special privileges and immunities.[111]

The concept of tax on means of transport provides for the option of tax preferences of an environmental character. Paid tax can be refunded if the taxpayers apply the combined transport approach (road transport alternated with rail transport). The amount of refunded tax depends on the number of rail trips of a given means of transport in the fiscal year. In the case of at least 100 trips in combined transport, the taxpayer qualifies for the refund of 100% of the amount of tax paid for the fiscal year. For the number of trips between 20 and 49, the refund is 25% of the amount of tax paid for the fiscal year.[112]

---

111 See more: B. Pahl, *Podatki o opłaty lokalne. Teoria i Praktyka*, Wolters Kluwer, Warsaw 2017, pp. 272–277.

112 J. Glumińska-Pawlic, *"Podatek od środków transportowych,"* [in:] *Prawo podatkowe*, ed. H. Dzwonkowski, C.H. Beck, Warsaw 2012, pp. 352–353.

Conclusion

This work outlines the basic theoretical issues and the main institutions of Polish tax law. A thorough review of the Polish taxation system goes beyond the scope of this book. The evolution of Polish tax law is marked by some unprecedented dynamics. We have witnessed numerous tax reforms and a variety of fiscal concepts, some of them never going further than the theory (not applicable to the legislative practice). Despite the positive assessment of the outcome of this nearly 30-year-long process, there are still many issues that court controversy and call for a reform. The most urging ones are briefly discussed in the following points:

I. No doubt, the instability and unpredictability of legislation is among the key challenges of the Polish tax system. For instance, the Act on Value Added Tax has been amended 70 times since entering into force on 1 May 2004. Such a large number of changes to this law has forced its double consolidation in the last 13 years. This picture is no more optimistic with other tax laws. For example, the 1993 Act on Corporate Income Tax has been amended over 200 times and the Act on Personal Income Tax, effective since 1 January 1992, nearly 300 times. Too frequent and often misguided changes have caused the laws to be incoherent and non-transparent. Considering that in Polish tax law the vast majority of tax obligations are constituted under the law, the consequences of the inconsistency and non-transparency of Polish tax law encumber taxpayers. The Polish legislator, to some extent confirming its impotence in this matter, has introduced the institution of fiscal interpretations in order to protect taxpayers from the effects of imperfect law (see Chapter 2). On the one hand, interpretations may be helpful for taxpayers, but, on the other, they expose the deficiencies of Polish tax law, not remedied even by numerous amendments. More than 35,000 individual interpretations are issued every year, and this number is growing. Another imperfection of Polish tax law is also a high level of bureaucracy in tax proceedings. It manifests itself in, for example, lengthy tax proceedings and court and administrative proceedings in tax matters. Economic operators suffer in the first place. Excessive bureaucracy in tax proceedings and the inconsistency of regulations is a double-edge sword as it also frustrates the attempts of tax authorities to combat tax avoidance. What follows, although the Tax Freedom Day calculated by the Polish economic think-tank Adam Smith Centre usually falls to mid-June (but it was no earlier than on 7 July in 2011), Poland reports a large tax gap. Only in 2015, the gap in the value added tax was 2.8% of gross domestic product (GDP). In contrast, the gap in corporate income tax in 2015 was less than EUR 10 billion, which was a good result against the European background. Although more effort has been taken since 2016 to curtail this problem (e.g. the general clause against tax avoidance or greater control of the so-called transfer prices), the Polish legislator, fiscal administration, and the doctrine of tax law are facing a major challenge on the way to reversing this trend.

II. Among more specific solutions found in individual tax types, the existing approaches are also debatable and call for adjustments. It seems that among indirect taxes, such as tax on goods and services, excise tax, and gambling tax, the primary objective is to maximise revenues from these taxes. It should be stressed that the maximisation of tax revenues is not to be achieved by increasing the tax burden but by closing the loopholes in tax law in such a way as to prevent tax avoidance. Some early attempts to do so have already been made. Having introduced more restrictive provisions on fuel trade, the fiscal efficiency in excise tax and value-added tax (VAT) is reported to be slowly enhancing. Similar measures have been implemented in tax on goods and services with a view to impairing the business of false tax refunds. Nevertheless, much still remains to be done. Bear in mind that the adoption of restrictive measures often affects ordinary taxpayers who, because of minor mistakes or oversights, are often treated on a par with entities misusing the law intentionally. As a follow-up, an in-depth research should be carried out to ensure that only those taxpayers who intentionally avoid taxes are held liable for their unlawful conduct. Additionally, it is worth considering whether the structure of excise tax should not include, to a greater extent than it is today, regulations addressing environmental protection issues.

As regards corporate income tax, the most urgent issue to resolve is the tax gap. The gap occurs mainly as a result of transferring income abroad through dividends. Some regulations aimed to curb this practice have already been implemented in income tax. From the taxpayer's viewpoint, among the drawbacks of regulations governing the rules of corporate income tax may be a phenomenon, known for more than ten years, of broadening the catalogue of tax revenues, which results in the extended scope of corporate taxation. This phenomenon coincides with the gradual narrowing of deductibles. Another thing is that taxpayers should be offered more flexible rules of amortisation/depreciation. Debatable is also the extensive list of exemptions regarding the object of taxation. They often seem to have been introduced ad hoc and without a deeper reflection on the desired shape of the levy. Apparently, in lieu of the extensive list of exemptions, the concept of income tax should be supplemented with such elements that would encourage taxpayers to invest their earned income.

Speaking of personal income tax, the correct determination of sources of income should be subject to a profound analysis. Presently, these sources are too many. This prevents the taxpayer from recognising their income correctly. Some of the taxpayer's revenues may, for example, fall within two or even three sources of income. A burning problem that has not been rectified for more than 25 years, and is not likely to be mitigated under tax law in the foreseeable future, is the exclusion of certain types of taxpayer's activity from income tax. This is the case in the traditional agricultural or forestry activities. Entities involved in this type of activity are charged with the fiscally ineffective agricultural and forest taxes. A thorough analysis should be given to the purpose of certain reliefs and exemptions in income tax. Some of them are out-of-date and no longer valid. A major problem is also low tax-free amount which by no means reflects the actual minimum subsistence (living wage). Judging by the legislator's approach, it should be noted that a serious drawback is the absence of statutory regulations forcing the automatic adjustment of tax thresholds, amounts of tax costs, or limits of exemptions and reliefs by the inflation level. Although the current annual inflation in Poland is negligible, given that the abovementioned taxation elements have not been valorised for several or even a dozen of years (when the accumulated inflation might have reached more than 10%), this is tantamount to increased fiscal burden invisible to taxpayers. It is also intriguing whether at the current stage of state development it is necessary for the tax system to offer simplified forms of taxation of income (revenue) earned by natural persons. It seems that today small economic operators can be supported in other ways.

Apparently, also the taxes intended for the municipal budget require a major reform. The arguments for the existence of inheritance and gift tax should be re-considered. Although there was a heated discussion on this tax more than 10 years ago, it was discontinued after the introduction of an exemption from tax on non-cash acquisition of property by taxpayers belonging to the immediate family. Perhaps following the Czech model, Poland should abolish inheritance and gift tax and tax the inherited property with personal income tax.

There are also many doubts about the real property taxation. Despite numerous attempts, no change has been implemented shifting real property taxation from the area-based system to the value-based system (*ad valorem*). There is no real cadastre system, no resources needed to perform value assessments of the existing real property, and no political will to implement the new approach because of little or no popularity of the system among the general public. Therefore, regardless of the value of immovable property, the tax burden is contingent upon the area of the estate. This state of affairs could be temporarily improved by the introduction, following the example of countries that do not have the *ad valorem* property taxation system, of some adjustment factors taking into account, for example, the location of the property. Another important drawback of the property, or actually landed property, taxation system is the existence of three land levies. Besides property tax, land can be subject to agricultural tax and forest tax. Both these taxes are the only levies imposed on entities conducting agricultural and forestry activities. They assume the role of wealth tax, one the one hand, and revenue tax, on the other. These taxes should be abolished and arable land and forests should be subject to property tax while the income from an agricultural and forestry activity should be burdened with income tax. Admittedly, the existence of these taxes known for their low fiscal efficiency adds to the already enormous complexity of the tax system.

Bibliography

Adamiak B., "*Wszczęcie postępowania,*" [in:] *Ordynacja podatkowa. Komentarz,* eds. B. Adamiak, J. Borkowski, P. Borszowski, R. Mastalski, J. Zubrzycki, Unimex, Wrocław 2017.

Babiarz S., Bogucki S., Dumas A., Pęk R., Presnarowicz S., Pustuł J., *Ryczałty w prawie podatkowym,* LexisNexis, Warsaw 2012.

Banasik P., Kałążny A., Morawski W., "Minimalny podatek dochodowy od wartości obiektów komercyjnych – wybrane problemy," *Przegląd Podatkowy* 2018, No. 2.

Bogucka-Felczak M., "*Zawieszenie postępowania,*" [in:] *Ordynacja podatkowa. Komentarz,* ed. H. Dzwonkowski, C.H. Beck, Warsaw 2016.

Borszowski P., "*Podatek leśny,*" [in:] *Podatki i opłaty lokalne. Podatek rolny. Podatek leśny. Komentarz,* eds. P. Borszowski, K. Stelmaszczyk, Wolters Kluwer, Warsaw 2016.

Brzeziński B., *Prawo podatkowe,* Dom organizatora, Toruń 2000a.

Brzeziński B., "Z problematyki ograniczenia możliwości uznania wydatku za koszt uzyskania przychodu," *Kwartalnik Prawa Podatkowego* 2000b, No. 1.

Brzeziński B., Filipczyk H., "*Nadpłata,*" [in:] *Nowelizacja Ordynacji podatkowej,* eds. B. Brzeziński, W. Morawski, Wolters Kluwer, Warsaw 2016.

Burzec M., "*Opodatkowanie nieruchomości,*" [in:] *Prawo podatkowe,* eds. P. Smoleń, W. Wójtowicz, C.H. Beck, Warsaw 2017a.

Burzec M., "*Podatek tonażowy,*" [in:] *Prawo podatkowe,* eds. P. Smoleń, W. Wójtowicz, C.H. Beck, Warsaw 2017b.

Burzec M., "*Taxation of Specialist Agricultural Activity in Poland – An Attempt to Evaluate the Existing Solutions,*" [in:] *Essential Problems with Taxation of Agriculture,* eds. M. Burzec, P. Smoleń, Wydawnictwo KUL, Lublin 2017c.

Chróścielewski W., Nykiel W., "*Postępowanie podatkowe,*" [in:] *Polskie prawo podatkowe,* ed. W. Nykiel, Difin, Warsaw 2013.

Chudzik M., "Zasady powstawania przychodów z działalności gospodarczej," *Monitor Podatkowy* 2006, No. 12.

Czajka Z., "*Pojęcie gospodarstwa rolnego na gruncie przepisów prawa podatkowego. Wybrane zagadnienia,*" [in:] *Pobór podatków samorządowych*, ed. A. Krukowski, Wydawnictwo KUL, Lublin 2011.

Dmoch W., *Podatek dochodowy od osób prawnych. Komentarz*, C.H. Beck, Warsaw 2017.

Duda-Hyz M., "Podatek od wydobycia niektórych kopalin – nowa jakość w polskim prawie podatkowym," *Ruch Prawniczy Ekonomiczny i Socjologiczny* 2013, No. 1.

Duda-Hyz M., "*Podatek od gier,*" [in:] *Prawo podatkowe*, eds. P. Smoleń, W. Wójtowicz, C.H. Beck, Warsaw 2017.

Dzwonkowski H., "Powstanie obowiązku podatkowego i przedawnienie prawa wymiaru zobowiązania," *Prawo i Podatki* 2009, No. 8.

Dzwonkowski H., "*Powstawanie obowiązku, wymiar i wykonywanie zobowiązań oraz roszczeń wynikających ze stosunków prawno podatkowych,*" [in:] *Prawo podatkowe*, ed. H. Dzwonkowski, C.H. Beck, Warsaw 2012.

Dzwonkowski H., Kondratowska J., "*Zabezpieczenie wykonania zobowiązań podatkowych,*" [in:] *Ordynacja podatkowa. Komentarz*, ed. H. Dzwonkowski, C.H. Beck, Warsaw 2016.

Dzwonkowski H., Kurzac M., "*Wygaśnięcie zobowiązań podatkowych*" [in:] *Ordynacja podatkowa. Komentarz*, ed. H. Dzwonkowski, C.H. Beck, Warsaw 2016.

Etel L., "*Podatki przychodowo-dochodowo-majątkowe,*" [in:] *System prawa finansowego. Prawo daninowe*, ed. L. Etel, Wolters Kluwer, Warsaw 2010.

Etel L., *Podatek od nieruchomości. Komentarz*, Wolters Kluwer, Warsaw 2012.

Filipczyk H., *Podatek od czynności cywilnoprawnych. Komentarz*, Wolters Kluwer, Warsaw 2015.

Gargul M., Oleś W., *Podatek od czynności cywilnoprawnych*, LexisNexis, Warsaw 2013.

Gil K., "*Art. 1 a [Podatkowa grupa kapitałowa],*" [in:] *Podatek dochodowy od osób prawnych. Komentarz*, K. Gil, A. Obońska, A. Wacławczyk, A. Walter, C.H. Beck, Warsaw 2017.

Glumińska-Pawlic J., "*Podatek od środków transportowych,*" [in:] *Prawo podatkowe,* ed. H. Dzwonkowski, C.H. Beck, Warsaw 2012.

Głuchowski J., Smoleń P., "Klasyfikacja podatników na gruncie ustawy o podatku od spadków i darowizn," *Gdańskie Studia Prawnicze* 2006, No. XVI.

Goettel A., *Podatkowoprawne skutki zawarcia i ustania małżeństwa,* Wolters Kluwer, Warsaw 2016.

Gomułowicz A., *Prawna formuła kosztu podatkowego,* Wolters Kluwer, Warsaw 2016.

Gorgol A., "*Podatek od wydobycia niektórych kopalin,*" [in:] *Prawo podatkowe,* eds. P. Smoleń, W. Wójtowicz, C.H. Beck, Warsaw 2017.

Hanusz A., "Strony postępowania podatkowego a ciężar dowodu," *Przegląd Podatkowy* 2004, No. 9.

Janiak B., "*Podatek od nieruchomości,*" [in:] *Opodatkowanie nieruchomości,* eds. T. Kosieradzki, R. Piekarz, B. Janiak, Wolters Kluwer, Warsaw 2016.

Kalinowski M., Masternak M., "*Doręczenia w postępowaniu podatkowym,*" [in:] *Nowelizacja Ordynacji podatkowej,* eds. B. Brzeziński, W. Morawski, Wolters Kluwer, Warsaw 2016.

Kandut K., "*Opodatkowanie dochodów nieujawnionych oraz potrzeba i kierunki ich zmian,*" [in:] *Potrzeba i kierunki reformy podatków dochodowych w Polsce,* ed. A. Pomorska, Wydawnictwo KUL, Lublin 2016.

Kandut K., *Opodatkowanie dochodów nieujawnionych jako narzędzie uszczelniające system podatkowy,* Wolters Kluwer, Warsaw 2017.

Karwat P., "*Powszechny podatek obrotowy – VAT,*" [in:] *Prawo podatkowe przedsiębiorców,* ed. H. Litwińczuk, Wolters Kluwer, Warsaw 2017.

Kleiber K., "Koszty uzyskania przychodów z tytułu zbycia nieruchomości," *Nieruchomości* 2015, No. 4.

Kosieradzki T., "*Najem,*" [in:] *Opodatkowanie nieruchomości,* eds. T. Kosieradzki, R. Piekarz, B. Janiak, Wolters Kluwer, Warsaw 2016.

Krawczyk I., "Podatek od czynności cywilnoprawnych a VAT," *Przegląd Podatkowy* 2001, No. 5.

Krok W., *Budowla w podatku od nieruchomości,* Wolters Kluwer, Warsaw 2010.

Kucia-Guściora B., *"Tax Residence in the Polish Personal Income Tax System – Major Problem Areas,"* [in:] *Selected Issues in Taxation and Tax Authorities in Central Europe*, ed. P. Smoleń, Wydawnictwo KUL, Lublin 2016.

Kucia-Guściora B., *"Podatek dochodowy od osób prawnych,"* [in:] *Prawo podatkowe*, eds. P. Smoleń, W. Wójtowicz, C.H. Beck, Warsaw 2017.

Litwińczuk H., *"Ustalanie dochodu przedsiębiorców. Zasady ogólne,"* [in:] *Prawo podatkowe przedsiębiorców*, ed. H. Litwińczuk, Wolters Kluwer, Warsaw 2017.

Małecki J., *"Państwowe podatki bezpośrednie,"* [in:] *Podatki i prawo podatkowe*, eds. A. Gomułowicz, J. Małecki, LexisNexis, Warsaw 2010a.

Małecki J., *"Postępowanie podatkowe w świetle Ordynacji podatkowej,"* [in:] *Podatki i prawo podatkowe*, eds. A. Gomułowicz, J. Małecki, LexisNexis, Warsaw 2010b.

Małecki J., *"Zobowiązania podatkowe w świetle Ordynacji podatkowej,"* [in:] *Podatki i prawo podatkowe*, eds. A. Gomułowicz, J. Małecki, LexisNexis, Warsaw 2010c.

Małecki P., Mazurkiewicz M., *CIT. Podatki i rachunkowość*, C.H. Beck, Warsaw 2017.

Marciniuk J., *Podatek dochodowy od osób fizycznych*, C.H. Beck, Warsaw 2017.

Mariuk A., Taudul A., *"Przychody z działalności wykonywanej osobiście,"* *Przegląd Podatkowy* 2004, No. 7.

Mastalski R., *Prawo podatkowe*, C.H. Beck, Warsaw 2017a.

Mastalski R., *"Ulgi w spłacie zobowiązań podatkowych,"* [in:] *Ordynacja podatkowa. Komentarz*, eds. B. Adamiak, J. Borkowski, P. Borszowski, R. Mastalski, J. Zubrzycki, Unimex, Wrocław 2017b.

Mastalski R., *"Zabezpieczenie wykonania zobowiązań podatkowych,"* [in:] *Ordynacja podatkowa. Komentarz*, eds. B. Adamiak, J. Borkowski, P. Borszowski, R. Mastalski, J. Zubrzycki, Unimex, Wrocław 2017c.

Masternak M., *"Nowe pojęcie strony postępowania podatkowego,"* *Przegląd Podatkowy* 2003, No. 3.

Matarewicz J., *Ustawa o podatku akcyzowym. Komentarz*, Wolters Kluwer, Warsaw 2016.

Matarewicz J., *Ustawa o podatku od towarów i usług. Komentarz*, C.H. Beck, Warsaw 2017.

Michalik T., *VAT Komentarz*, C.H. Beck, Warsaw 2017.

Michta D., Pankrac L., *Ustawa o podatku od czynności cywilnoprawnych. Komentarz*, LexisNexis, Warsaw 2013.

Militz M., "Nowe zasady powstawania obowiązku podatkowego w VAT – ułatwienia czy utrudnienia?," *Przegląd Podatkowy* 2014, No. 2.

Militz M., "Odwrotne obciążenie w VAT – wymogi materialne i formalne realizacji prawa do odliczenia podatku naliczonego," *Przegląd Podatkowy* 2018, No. 3.

Morawski W., Janicki T., "*Urzędowe interpretacje prawa podatkowego*," [in:] *Nowelizacja Ordynacji podatkowej*, eds. B. Brzeziński, W. Morawski, Wolters Kluwer, Warsaw 2016.

Ofiarski Z., *Ogólne prawo podatkowe. Zagadnienia materialnoprawne i proceduralne*, LexisNexis, Warsaw 2010.

Olesińska A., Prejs E., "*Odpowiedzialność osób trzecich za zobowiązania podatkowe*," [in:] *Nowelizacja Ordynacji podatkowej*, eds. B. Brzeziński, W. Morawski, Wolters Kluwer, Warsaw 2016.

Pahl B., *Podatki i opłaty lokalne. Teoria i Praktyka*, Wolters Kluwer, Warsaw 2017.

Parulski S., *Akcyza. Komentarz*, Wolters Kluwer, Warsaw 2016.

Pietrasiewicz W., Romańczuk M., *Koszty uzyskania przychodów*, C.H. Beck, Warsaw 2009.

Pogoński M., *Koszty uzyskania przychodów w podatkach dochodowych (PIT, CIT)*, C.H. Beck, Warsaw 2014.

Pogoński M., "*Zakres kosztów uzyskania przychodów w związku z odpłatnym zbyciem papierów wartościowych*," *Monitor Podatkowy* 2015, No. 7.

Presnarowicz S., "*Kary porządkowe*," [in:] *Ordynacja podatkowa. Komentarz*, ed. L. Etel, Wolters Kluwer, Warsaw 2017.

Radzikowski K., "Pojęcie przychodu należnego z działalności gospodarczej w ustawach podatkowych," *Przegląd Prawa Publicznego* 2009, No. 11.

Ryszard K., "*Podatek od gier*," [in:] *Gry hazardowe. Komentarz do ustawy o grach hazardowych*, eds. M. Bik, R. Kamionowski, D. Obrępalski, K. Ryszard, C.H. Beck, Warsaw 2013.

Smoleń P., *Kształtowanie obciążenia w podatku od spadków i darowizn*, Wydawnictwo KUL, Lublin 2006.

Smoleń P., *"Podatki samorządowe,"* [in:] *Prawo podatkowe – część ogólna i szczegółowa*, eds. W. Wójtowicz, C.H. Beck, Warsaw 2009.

Smoleń P., *"Podatki majątkowe,"* [in:] *System prawa finansowego. Prawo daninowe*, ed. L. Etel, Wolters Kluwer, Warsaw 2010.

Smoleń P., *"Podatek od spadków i darowizn,"* [in:] *Prawo podatkowe*, eds. P. Smoleń, W. Wójtowicz, C.H. Beck, Warsaw 2017.

Smoleń P., *"Organy podatkowe,"* [in:] *Ordynacja podatkowa. Komentarz*, ed. H. Dzwonkowski, C.H. Beck, Warsaw 2018.

Stachurski W., *"Zabezpieczenie wykonania zobowiązań podatkowych,"* [in:] *Ordynacja podatkowa. Komentarz*, ed. L. Etel, Wolters Kluwer, Warsaw 2017.

Strzelec D., *Opodatkowanie przychodów nieznajdujących pokrycia w nieujawnionych źródłach przychodu lub pochodzących ze źródeł nieujawnionych*, C.H. Beck, Warsaw 2015.

Styczyński R., *Wynagrodzenia pracownicze i inne przychody*, Difin, Warsaw 2015.

Szustek-Janowska M., *"Zobowiązania podatkowe,"* [in:] *Prawo podatkowe-część ogólna i szczegółowa*, ed. W. Wójtowicz, C.H. Beck, Warsaw 2009.

Teszner K., *"Interpretacje przepisów prawa podatkowego,"* [in:] *Ordynacja podatkowa. Komentarz*, ed. L. Etel, Wolters Kluwer, Warsaw 2017.

Wojewoda-Buraczyńska K., "Zmiany w podatku tonażowym," *Przegląd Prawa publicznego* 2015, No. 3.

Zdanowicz J., "Zwolnienia w podatku od spadków i darowizn," *Monitor Podatkowy* 1999, No. 12.

Zdebel M., *"Prawa i obowiązki następców prawnych oraz podmiotów przekształconych,"* [in:] *Ordynacja podatkowa. Komentarz*, ed. H. Dzwonkowski, C.H. Beck, Warsaw 2016.

Lex et Res Publica
Polish Legal and Political Studies

Edited by
Anna Jaroń

www.peterlang.com